Crossing the River

The contribution of spirituality to humanity and its future

Edited by
Arthur Hawes with Ben Bano

Crossing the River: The contribution of spirituality to humanity and its future

© Arthur Hawes with Ben Bano

The authors have asserted their rights in accordance with the Copyright, Designs and Patents Act (1988) to be identified as the authors of this work.

Published by:
Pavilion Publishing and Media Ltd
Rayford House
School Road
Hove
East Sussex
BN3 5HX
Tel: 01273 434 943
Fax: 01273 227 308
Email: info@pavpub.com
Web: www.pavpub.com

Published 2014.

A catalogue record for this book is available from the British Library.

Print ISBN: 978-1-909810-65-5
EPDF ISBN: 978-1-909810-66-2
EPUB ISBN: 978-1-909810-67-9
MOBI ISBN: 978-1-909810-68-6

Pavilion is the leading training and development provider and publisher in the health, social care and allied fields, providing a range of innovative training solutions underpinned by sound research and professional values. We aim to put our customers first, through excellent customer service and value.

Editors: Arthur Hawes with Ben Bano
Production editor: Catherine Ansell-Jones, Pavilion Publishing and Media Ltd
Cover design: Phil Morash, Pavilion Publishing and Media Ltd
Page layout and typesetting: Phil Morash, Pavilion Publishing and Media Ltd
Printing: CMP Digital Print Solutions

'Through wood and dale the sacred river ran,
Then reached the caverns measureless to man.'

Samuel Taylor Coleridge, Kubla Khan (1816)

Royalties for this book
will be donated to the
Motor Neurone Disease Association.

Contents

Peter Gilbert 2

Contributors 4

Preface *by Kevin Taggart* 13

Introduction *by Arthur Hawes* 15

Spirituality and mental health

Chapter 1: The clue: to improve mental health services the
client must be central to the whole enterprise 19
Arthur Hawes

Chapter 2: The running group 29
Qaisra Khan

Chapter 3: Breathing out – breathing in 35
John Swinton

Chapter 4: Recovery and spirituality: how the church and healthcare
can develop more faith – in each other 43
Antony Sheehan

Chapter 5: Life is a mystery to be lived, not a problem to be solved: mental
health as an adventure and journey 53
Stephan Ball

Spirituality and social care

Chapter 6: Living and breathing spirituality in social work and social care..............67
Margaret Holloway

Chapter 7: It's humanity, stoopid! Humanity, spirituality and
social work education 77
Bernard Moss

Chapter 8: Spirituality, listening to the service user's story,
compassion and an ethic of care 87
Margaret McGettrick

Chapter 9: Modelling well-being in social care 95
Hári Sewell

Spirituality and interfaith relations

Chapter 10: The Gilbert pilgrimage 105
Martin Aaron

Chapter 11: Dying to live: graduating from the University of Life 113
Chetna Kang

Chapter 12: Spirituality, Buddhism and psychological therapies –
a perspective 119
Sarajane Aris

Spirituality and leadership

Chapter 13: The river's flow: life and leadership personified 131
Bhai Sahib Dr Mohinder Singh

Chapter 14: Cynicism, leadership and integrity....................137
Peter Sedgwick

Chapter 15: Leadership in learning disability services 145
Peter Bates

Chapter 16: In my end is my beginning.................................155
Ben Bano

Further reading..163

Peter Gilbert

15 April 1950 – 12 December 2013

It was a moment of great sadness when I heard the news of Peter's death on 12th December 2013. Peter had been battling with motor neurone disease since the initial diagnosis in November 2012 and everyone who knew him admired his courage as he coped with this most pernicious of diseases.

Peter and Sue have three children and one grandson, who is very special. At the age of 18, Peter joined the army and went to the Royal Military Academy at Sandhurst and, while there, went up to Balliol College, Oxford, to read modern history. After university, he became a trainee social worker and ended his professional social work career as director of social services for Worcestershire. From 2001 he was deeply involved in the Spirituality Programme. He used every obvious avenue to articulate his spirituality and particularly through his own Catholic faith community where he was not only highly regarded, but had also been instrumental in persuading the Catholic bishops to take spirituality and mental health seriously, to a point where they have now appointed their own adviser. Peter's own interests in spirituality moved far beyond the world of mental health and included areas such as spirituality and leadership. He wrote extensively about spirituality and, as well as editing books and writing papers, he wrote a number of books himself.

Peter was a member of the BASS (British Association for the Study of Spirituality) executive committee and the editorial board of the *Journal for the Study of Spirituality*. He contributed to the journal, often with book reviews and to BASS biennial conferences, especially with his meditations.

Peter was emeritus professor of social work and spirituality at Staffordshire University, and visiting professor with the University of Worcester. Peter was the NIMHE project lead on spirituality from its inception until 31st March 2008, when the work transferred to the National Spirituality and Mental Health Forum. Peter became the National Lead for the Forum and also from 2008–2010 he was chair of the National Development for Inclusion and visiting professor at the Birmingham and Solihull Foundation NHS Trust, leading their spirituality research programme. Between 2003 and 2008 he was NIMHE/CSIP Fellow in Social Care. In recent months Peter received several honours to mark his unique contribution to health and social care and interfaith relations.

Signed up to ensuring the integration of theory with practice, Peter was an associate member of ADASS, and wrote the national ADSS/NIMHE guidance on the integration of mental health services. In 2008 he published *Guidelines on Spirituality for Staff in Acute Care Services*. He was national facilitator for the National Social Care Strategic Network.

Peter published *Leadership: Being effective and remaining human* in 2005, and he and his co-editors published *Spirituality, Values and Mental Health: Jewels for the journey* (2007). He was a co-editor of *The International Journal of Leadership in Public Services*. His most recent publications are *Social Work and Mental Health: The value of everything* (with colleagues) in 2010; leadership and supervision development packs, with Dr Neil Thompson; and a chapter on his own experience of mental distress in Basset and Stickley's *Voices of Experience: Narratives of survival and mental health* (2010). The Pavilion handbooks *Spirituality and Mental Health* and *Spirituality and End of Life Care* were published in 2011 and 2013 respectively.

Whenever Peter was presenting spirituality, whether for a conference of 200 people or a seminar for 20 professionals, he always made the point that he had experienced mental health problems himself and so understood the user perspective from within. Everyone in the field of spirituality owes Peter a great debt of gratitude for his unerring courage in driving forward a not always popular area of human concern, his strong work ethic, his readiness to be available to a whole range of people, his amazing ability to network, and his stoicism in the face of adversity. He will ever be unique.

May he rest in peace, grow in love and rise in glory.

Arthur Hawes, December 2013

Contributors

Antony Sheehan

Professor Antony Sheehan was the 2011–2012 Health Foundation Quality Improvement Fellow at the Institute for Healthcare Improvement (IHI) in Boston. Before studying at IHI he was the chief executive officer of one of England's largest community health services that provides mental health, learning disability, primary care and other community health services for a population of over one million people. He has been a prominent figure in developing NHS services in England for more than a decade and a half.

From 1999 to 2007 Antony worked in the UK Government as a senior civil servant heading an important group within the Department of Health. His responsibilities as director general included policy for mental health; maternity and families; children's health care; healthcare in the criminal justice system; and older people's services.

Antony is a nurse by background and has worked in practice, education, and management. He is currently a visiting professor in the School of Public Health at The University of Memphis and was recently appointed to the position of President of The Church Health Centre in Memphis, Tennessee. This is America's largest faith-based health clinic and serves the uninsured working poor.

Arthur Hawes

Arthur Hawes is Archdeacon Emeritus of Lincoln and Canon of the cathedral, following his retirement in 2008. He was founder chairman of the North Worcestershire Association Mind, following post-graduate work at Birmingham University. From 1976–1992 he was a chaplain at acute psychiatric units in Norwich and from 1986–1995 he was a Mental Health Act commissioner.

From 1995–2010, Arthur was chair of the Church of England's Mental Health Advisory Group. As a member of the Mission and Public affairs Council, he presented two debates in the General Synod of the Church of England on mental health issues. In 1996 he was made Jubilee Patron of Mind and in 1999 he was a member of Mind's National Reference Group. From 1998–2006 he was non-executive director of the mental health trust in Lincolnshire and he was a member of the NHS Confederation Mental Health Policy Committee from 2003–2007. From 2003–2005 he was chairman of the East Midlands NIMHE Regional Development Centre and member of the criminal justice mental health research group at Lincoln University from 2007–2010. From 2006–2008 he was appointed Mental Health Act advisor to the Lincolnshire Partnership Trust and in 2008 he was appointed as training consultant to the Trust. He became a member of the National Spirituality and Mental Health Forum in 2003 and was a co-chairman of the Forum from 2009–2011; he is now its secretary.

Arthur has been a visiting fellow of Staffordshire University and is one of two vice presidents of the British Association for the Study of Spirituality. He has published many occasional papers, edited *The Anne French Memorial Lectures* and contributed to a number of publications on theology, spirituality and mental health.

Ben Bano

Ben Bano has been a social worker for 40 years and most recently worked as director of social care and older people's services in the East Kent Mental Health Trust. Following his retirement in 2005, he established Telos Training Ltd. with a particular focus on training in spirituality and mental health, as well as the Welcome Me as I Am project, which focuses on raising mental health awareness in faith communities. Ben saw Peter Gilbert very much as his mentor in taking forward his work over the last few years. He is currently co-vice chair of the National Spirituality and Mental Health Forum and secretary of the Mental Health Social Work Strategic Network, of which Peter Gilbert was a founder member. He has contributed chapters to several of Peter Gilbert's books, including the most recent publication *Spirituality and End of Life Care* (2013).

Bernard Moss

Bernard Moss is emeritus professor of social work education and spirituality at Staffordshire University, where he developed the involvement of service users and carers in communication skills training for social work students. His innovative approach won two national awards for service user involvement. His teaching areas include bereavement and loss, and social work values. As a university teacher his excellence has been recognised by the Higher Education Academy, who awarded him a national teaching fellowship and then a senior fellowship. Bernard's interest in spirituality was grounded in his own faith-community leadership, but while at Staffordshire University he led the way in demonstrating not only the importance of this topic to social work education and practice, but also how it could be creatively included and explored in the social work curriculum. For this developmental work he was awarded his PhD in 2011.

Bernard has published widely on the theme of spirituality, most notably by co-authoring, with professor Margaret Holloway, *Spirituality and Social Work* (2010). Currently, he is developing his interest in using labyrinth walks to explore mindfulness, creativity and spirituality, and leads workshops in a wide variety of contexts using his portable labyrinth.

Bhai Sahib Mohinder Singh

Bhai Sahib Mohinder Singh serves as third in the line of spiritual leaders who have guided the work of Guru Nanak Nishkam Sewak Jatha UK (GNNSJ). This is a Sikh faith-based organisation with its international headquarters in Handsworth, Birmingham, dedicated to 'selfless service' in the name of the founder of the five-centuries-old Sikh faith.

Since being appointed to serve in 1995, Bhai Sahib has spearheaded and supported a wide range of local and global projects and partnerships, involving extensive civic, interfaith and intra-faith engagement. Building on the legacy of his two predecessors, Bhai Sahib's credentials and distinctive style of leadership combine 'heritage conservation' with 'social innovation' by imbuing and bringing 'fragrance' to these multifaceted developments through an ethos of putting spiritual values into action. This for him is enabled by a deepening of one's engagement with faith itself.

A civil and structural engineer by profession, Bhai Sahib has some 27 years of experience in planning housing developments in Kenya and Zambia. At the age of 50, he took early retirement, answering an inner calling to devote the rest of his life to selfless service amongst a new community of first-generation Sikhs settling in the UK, guided to revitalise their faith with meaning and purpose in new contexts.

The title 'Bhai Sahib' suggests a respected, brotherly leader; it is also an official title bestowed upon him by the highest Sikh authority in 2010, recognising his historic contributions to the Sikh faith internationally. Bhai Sahib's work to promote co-operation and collaboration for peace and human flourishing are widely recognised through a host of chairmanships, trusteeships, directorships and patronships.

Bhai Sahib holds honorary doctorates from the University of Central England (2002) and the University of Birmingham (2006) for services to religious faith propagation, community service and educational research. He is an

'Interfaith Visionary', recipient of the Juliet Hollister Award from the Temple of Understanding (2008), whose past awardees have included His Holiness the Dalai Lama and the late Nelson Mandela. In 2012 Bhai Sahib became the first Sikh to receive a Papal Knighthood of St Gregory the Great from Pope Benedict XVI. He is a member of the Elijah Board of World's Religious Leaders (EBWRL) and the European Council of Religious Leaders (ECRL) and was an ex-advisor on the Fetzer Institute's Council of Religions and Spirituality.

Two of Bhai Sahib's major current projects include planning for the Museum of World's Religions in Birmingham, and an international Charter for Forgiveness.

Bhai Sahib also inspires and capacity-builds members of his faith community to provide an anchor of regeneration for the wider local community in Handsworth. This includes shaping new infrastructures and models to promote holistic well-being, community volunteering, education, healthcare of the young and elderly, including a focus on Sikh chaplaincy and mental and spiritual health, through which Bhai Sahib and Peter Gilbert were first introduced.

Chetna Kang

Dr Chetna Kang MBBS MRCPsych is a consultant psychiatrist, pastor in the Bhakti Yoga tradition of Hinduism, radio broadcaster and current co-chair of The National Spirituality and Mental Health Forum. She has spent more than 15 years studying, applying and presenting the Vedic Paradigm and its relationship with well-being to a wide audience ranging from healthcare professionals, bankers and academics right through to her temple congregation, using various media such as seminars, journals, books, radio and television. She worked with Peter Gilbert on the National Spirituality and Mental Health Project from 2006.

Hári Sewell

Hári Sewell is founder and director of HS Consultancy and is a former executive director of health and social care in the NHS, where his responsibilities included learning and development and organisational development. He is a writer and speaker in his specialist areas of equalities in mental health.

Hári is author of *Working with Ethnicity Race and Culture in Mental Health: A handbook for practitioners* (2009) and his latest edited book *The Equality Act 2010 in Mental Health* was published by Jessica Kingsley Publishers in November 2012.

John Swinton

John Swinton is professor in practical theology and pastoral care in the School of Divinity, History and Philosophy at the University of Aberdeen. He has a background in mental health nursing and healthcare chaplaincy and has researched and published extensively within the areas of practical theology, mental health, spirituality and human well-being, and the theology of disability. He is the director of Aberdeen University's Centre for Spirituality, Health and Disability, and co-director of the University's Kairos Forum. His publications include *Dementia: Living in the memories of God* (2012), *Raging with Compassion: Pastoral responses to the problem of evil* (2007) and *Spirituality in Mental Health Care: Rediscovering a 'forgotten' dimension* (2001).

Margaret Holloway

Margaret Holloway is professor of social work at the University of Hull and a qualified social worker. She directs the Centre for Spirituality Studies and the Centre for End of Life Studies, and from 2009–2013 she acted as social care lead on the UK National End of Life Care Programme. Margaret is a founder member of the British Association for the Study of Spirituality and former vice-chair. She researches death, dying and bereavement, with a particular interest in spiritual and philosophical issues and transcultural approaches. She also undertakes research into social aspects of chronic illness and the delivery of health and social care services for frail older people. Amongst her many publications are *Negotiating Death in Contemporary Health and Social Care* (2007), with Bernard Moss, *Spirituality and Social Work* (2010) and with Steve Nolan, *A-Z of Spirituality* (2013).

Margaret McGettrick

Margaret currently works as a part-time lay Roman Catholic chaplain at St. Bernard's Hospital, for the West London Mental Health NHS Trust. She also co-ordinates the care of the sick and housebound and runs a mental health support group in her local church community in Redhill, Surrey.

Margaret was a trained registered nurse for over 30 years. She has degrees in social administration and healthcare chaplaincy and is currently studying for an MA in pastoral theology. She has a special interest in spirituality and healing prayer ministry.

Margaret's career spans social work, community development, nursing and healthcare chaplaincy. In 1979, while working for Toc H, she was instrumental in establishing a hospice programme of care in Johannesburg, Southern Africa.

She is currently vice chairman and trustee of the National Spirituality and Mental Health Forum. She is also a member of the Roman Catholic Bishop's Conference of England and Wales, Mental Health Reference Group.

Martin Aaron

Martin Aaron originally qualified as an accountant and founded his own corporate consultancy practice from which he retired in 2011. Martin has held a great interest in mental health and religious issues since his teens and has spent a major part of his life as a volunteer in the mental health field.

During the last 20 years he extended his interest in mental health particularly through his interfaith work and spirituality. In furtherance of his concern he became a member of the Advisory Council of the Three Faiths Forum (a national forum of the three Abrahamic faiths) and co-chaired its medical group. He founded and chaired The Jewish Society for the Mentally Handicapped in 1976 and was later a trustee for many years of the merged Ravenswood Foundation (now Norwood, of which HM the Queen is patron, the organisation provides residential care and services for people with learning disabilities).

Extending his interest across the whole spectrum of mental health, in 1989 he founded The Jewish Association for Mental Illness, (JAMI) of which he remains honorary life president. JAMI is now the largest Jewish mental health service provider in the UK. Martin served on the advisory committees on both MIND and MENCAP in the 1980s.

During the mid-1990s he was invited to join a working group on religion and mental health at the former Health Education Authority. In 2003 he was invited to take over the chair and subsequently registered the religion, mental health and spirituality group as a separate registered multi-faith charity under the title The National Spirituality and Mental Health Forum. Since the Forum was established he worked closely with Peter Gilbert who played an important part in its development. In 2007 he was invited to become a visiting professor at the Faculty of Health at Staffordshire University, a position he still holds.

In 2011 The British Association for the Study of Spirituality was registered and Martin became its honorary treasurer. Martin has been involved in research and has served on several government department consultative committees over many years; he has organised, chaired and presented at numerous conferences on mental health, religion and spirituality topics. He has written many papers and has appeared on radio and TV on several occasions. For 11 years Martin served as a mentor for The Prince's Trust.

In addition to his academic and professional qualifications, Martin is a life fellow of The Royal Society of Arts and a life fellow of The Royal Society of Medicine.

Peter Bates

Peter Bates works for NDTi, a non-profit agency that offers consultancy to mental health and learning disability services; and for Nottingham University, where he promotes patient and public involvement in co-producing health research. He previously worked in probation, employment service, social services, the NHS and auditing. He has published 80 items in the areas of employment, disability, empowerment and inclusion and is in constant demand as a lively and effective trainer. Peter is married to a teacher and for the last 35 years they have been active members of St Nicholas Church in Nottingham.

Peter Sedgwick

Peter Sedgwick was policy officer on home affairs for the Church of England from 1996–2004. In this brief he covered the area of mental health, and worked closely with Peter Gilbert. Since 2004 he has been principal of St. Michael's College, Cardiff; lecturer in theology at Cardiff University; and ministry officer for the church in Wales.

Qaisra Khan

Qaisra Khan has worked across the public sector both as a volunteer and in a paid capacity. Her roles have included social services inspector for the Department of Health, non-executive director, local authority councillor, school governor, and spiritual and cultural care co-ordinator. She has been a freelance consultant since 2000, working on a variety of contracts including spiritual care, and as a speaker and facilitator.

Her education includes an MA in Islamic Cultures and Societies from the School of African and Oriental Studies, University of London, and BA (Joint Honours) History and Archaeology from St David's University College, University of Wales. The BA involved a year studying Christian theology.

Qaisra has contributed to the publications *Spirituality and Mental Health: A handbook* (2011), *Understanding Wellbeing* (2011), *Faith Initiative* (2012), *Nurturing the Nation: The Asian contribution to the NHS since 1948* (2013).

Sarajane Aris

Sarajane Aris is a consultant clinical psychologist, and founder and director of Aris Consulting, Coaching and Psychological Services Ltd. She was head of adult psychology services for Derbyshire Healthcare Foundation Trust for 10 years and director of policy for the British Psychological Society's division of clinical psychology 2012/13. She has worked within the NHS for over 30 years.

She has been the national lead for spirituality for the British Psychological Society since 2002, and has worked with Peter Gilbert on various aspects of the National Spirituality and Mental Health Project since 2002. She has been the psychology representative on the National Mental Health and Spirituality Forum since this time and was responsible for setting up Derbyshire Mental Healthcare Foundation Trust's Spirituality Strategy and Steering Group (2009–11).

She founded the Transpersonal Network for Clinical and Counselling Psychologists and therapists in the UK (1997–2011), has been involved in organisational change and development work for a variety of organisations such as Avon and Wiltshire Mental Health Partnership NHS Trust, the Cancer Help Centre, now the Penny Brohn Centre, Bristol, amongst others.

She has been following Tibetan Buddhist training for the past 10 years with Sogyal Rinpoche and seeks to integrate her practice into daily life. Her life is informed by the principles of love, wisdom and compassion.

Sarajane has contributed various chapters to books on consciousness and spirituality in mental health. She is co-author of the second edition of *Counselling and Helping* with Professor Richard Velleman (2010), which includes a chapter on spirituality and helping.

Stephan Ball

Stephan Ball has worked in mental health for 30 years mostly as a community mental health nurse and care co-ordinator in the community in Britain and also in Aotearoa/New Zealand. He has contributed to mental health nursing conferences and papers in New Zealand. He has a degree in social sciences and a diploma in psychotherapy.

Stephan is a past chairperson of Being Alongside, a small mental health and spirituality charity bringing together service users, carers, pastoral workers, professionals and volunteers. He is also a trustee of the National Forum for Spirituality and Mental Health.

Stephan is a Quaker with an interest in ecumenical, interfaith, environmental and social justice matters. He is involved in various projects to do with mental health and distress in the Quaker and wider community.

Preface

Peter's secondary education took place at Worth in Sussex, a school run by Benedictine monks. For many years afterwards he took an active part in the lay community of St. Benedict, an organisation founded by Worth Abbey for lay people who wish to keep closely in touch with the Abbey and with Benedictine spirituality. Inevitably, therefore, Peter's outlook on leadership and community living were influenced by what he found in studying St. Benedict's Rule for monks, and by what he experienced from this close association with monastic life at and through Worth Abbey.

The wisdom contained in St. Benedict's Rule is applicable for any age and many circumstances. Peter discovered this, and was able to put it to very good use in his key contribution to the themes in his books – leadership, mental health, social care and interfaith relations. And what is that wisdom?

Firstly, the leader must be a person of integrity: *'To be worthy of the task of governing a monastery, the abbot must always remember what his title signifies and act as a superior would ... The abbot must always remember what he is and remember what he is called, aware that more will be expected of a man to whom more has been entrusted'*. Peter's contribution to a truly human and authentic approach to leadership is based on this maxim.

Secondly, the leader must have a real concern for each individual: *'It is the abbot's responsibility to have great concern and to act with all speed, discernment and diligence in order not to lose any of the sheep entrusted to him. He should realise that he has undertaken care of the sick, not tyranny over the healthy ... He must accommodate and adapt himself to each one's character...'* Peter has integrated this wisdom into all that he has achieved to show how organisations which put individual staff in the forefront are likely to be effective and provide better outcomes for those who use their services. Concern and respect for individuals has always been at the heart of his warm relations with other faiths.

Thirdly, the leader must seek the advice of others: *'As often as anything important is to be done in the monastery, the abbot shall call the whole community together and himself explain what the business is; and thereafter hearing the advice of the brothers, let him ponder it and follow what he judges the wiser course.'* Using this maxim, he has always emphasised the need for effective leaders and organisations to give time and space to ensure that individual concerns are heard if organisations such as NHS trusts are not to become dysfunctional.

Integrity, compassion, a listening ear: these are qualities which St. Benedict looks for in a monastic leader, qualities which Peter, I believe, came to appreciate, value and use in his unique contribution to the areas covered in this most welcome book.

Kevin Taggart
Abbot of Worth 2010–2013

Introduction

Arthur Hawes

'And I saw brightness, in the form of a river, shining, amber, between banks pricked out with miraculous spring. Living sparks flashed from this river, and fell into the blossoms on all sides, like gold-set rubies.'

Dante's Paradiso, Canto XXX, The River of Light

The 15th of May 2013 was an important day. This is because I met Ben Bano in the House of Lords at the launch of a research report from the Mental Health Foundation on the mental health of the baby boomer generation. We began talking about Peter and the pernicious illness that was crippling him. We wondered how we might honour the incredible contribution he has made to the world of spirituality and simultaneously suggested writing a book which would capture his work and ideas and encourage others to continue, develop and research the role of spirituality in the 21st century. We appreciated just how comprehensive Peter's grasp of the subject was and commented on his nomenclature at the end of every email. This listed his current roles and often ran to seven or eight lines!

We were delighted when Pavilion agreed to publish the book and that Peter knew about this in detail and about all who would be contributing. Not only are the contributors experts in their own right, but they are also multidisciplinary and multi-faith. The book is very much a Forum (The National Forum for Spirituality and Mental Health)[1] project because Peter was its project officer for five years after the National Institute for Mental Health in England (later CSIP) project became regionalised.

There is a certain irony running throughout the book which, in a sense, captures the essence of Peter and his work, as will become apparent as the book unfolds. Peter's last book published by Pavilion was *Spirituality and End of Life Care* (2013). It was published as he was nearing the end of his life.

Motor neurone disease invariably attacks the respiratory system. The Greek word for 'air' is also the word for spirit. It is incredibly ironic that the illness which robbed him of his life is inextricably linked to the subject he pioneered – spirituality. Lastly, Peter was an avid runner, which depends upon a healthy

---

1 There is a full description of Peter's association with the Forum and his work in the world of spirituality on the Forum website: http://www.mhspirituality.org.uk/

respiratory system. As a result he was very fit and always counted running as an integral part of his spirituality. It has given rise to a number of phrases. For example, Sue described his last days as 'Peter's final lap'.

The title of this book deserves an explanation. In the summer of 2013 I received an email from Peter soon after he and Sue had met with the doctor from the hospice in Worcester and the subject of the email was 'Crossing the River'. It seemed natural to use this as the title of the book. It was in the hospice that Peter sadly died just before Christmas last year. In the spring of 2012 the Forum vice chairman, Christopher Jones, sadly died. In his work for the Church of England and other organisations, he operated very much in parallel with Peter. Later, Jenny (Christopher's widow) said that she hoped Christopher would be there to meet Peter when he crossed the river. It is this very real shared belief in eternity that not only sums up Peter but is also a natural expression of his and Christopher's spirituality.

Ben and I agreed it was important to create a book that would encapsulate the four main areas of Peter's work. They are:

- spirituality and leadership

- spirituality and social care

- spirituality and mental health

- spirituality and interfaith relations.

The four themes are not grouped together but rather, because they are cross cutting, are liberally spread throughout the book. The contributors, whose biographies are to be found on pages 4–12, were asked at the beginning of their chapter if they would kindly make a personal reference to Peter and draw on a thought or comment of his which could then be expanded.

I am particularly grateful to all the contributors and, not least, Ben Bano who has been a huge support to me. I am grateful to Kerry Boettcher and Catherine Ansell-Jones and their team at Pavilion for their encouragement, help and advice. Lastly I am very grateful to two wives. Sue Gilbert has followed the progress of the book with her indomitable spirit at a time when Peter was very ill and dying and my own wife, Melanie, has been alongside me reading, commenting and advising.

I hope every reader will be stimulated by the book and want to continue and develop their own interests in spirituality. I also hope it is a fitting tribute to Peter, which honours his work over many years and in many parts of the UK.

Spirituality and
mental health

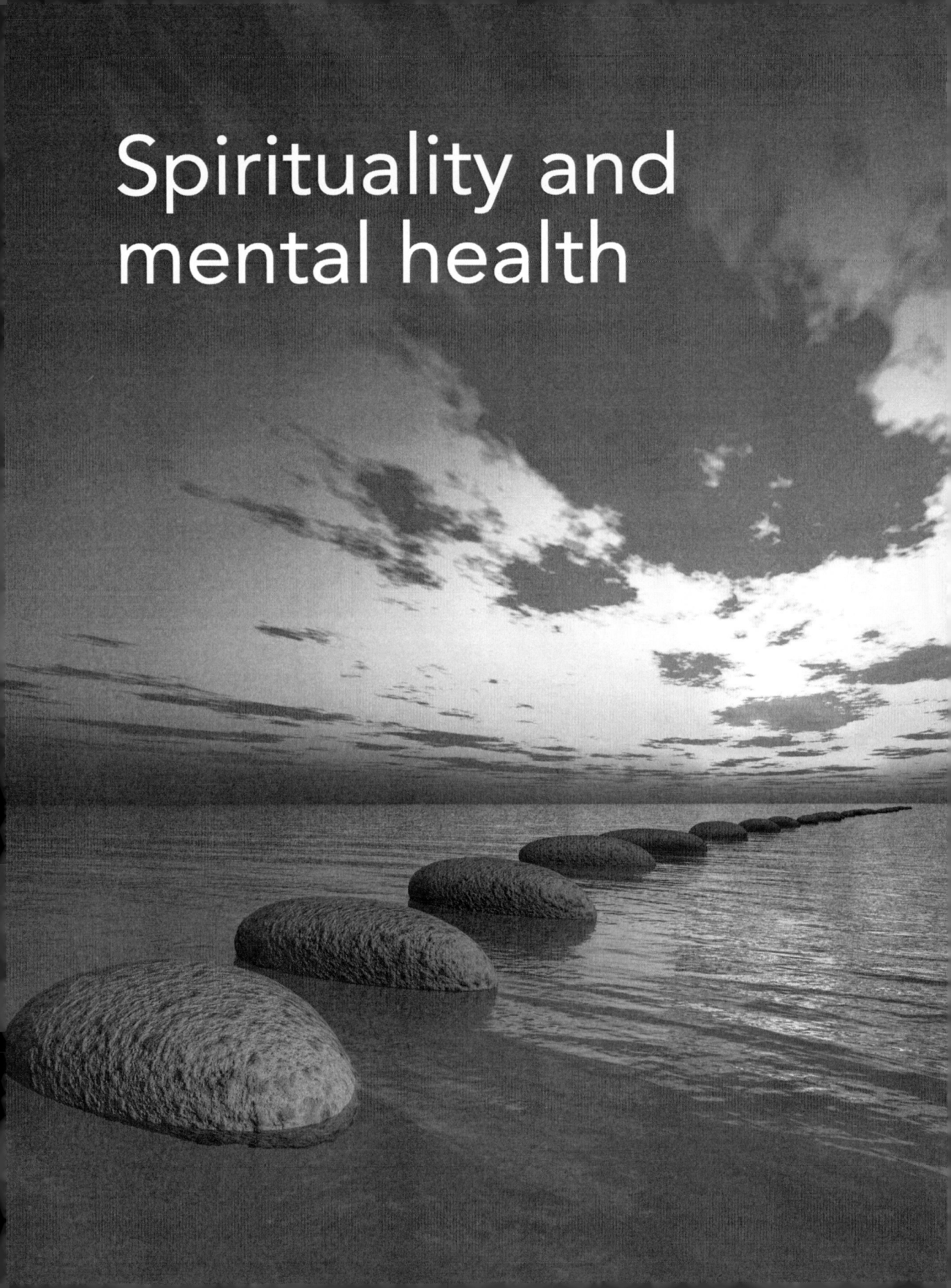

Chapter 1: The clue: to improve mental health services the client must be central to the whole enterprise

Arthur Hawes

So much of the planning, development, and financing of the NHS is directed towards the acute, surgical and medical, and primary care services. This is understandable because of the pressure to deliver at the point of perceived need. In the acute phase there is nothing to compare with the service provided by the NHS. However, it struggles with the demands of rehabilitation, continuing care and post-acute convalescence. A recent development has been to encourage those who use the service to become more active and involved in their own health, with the result that the passive and uncomplaining patient has been replaced by the more proactive service user.

In the world of mental health, the patient became much more proactive with the introduction of new mental health legislation – the Mental Health Act – in 1983 and amended in 2007. The development of the legislation is something I will return to later. It was not so very long ago that a person with mental health problems was admitted to hospital as a patient who, without consent, could be medicated, treated electrically and even leucotomised.

Peter Gilbert, in any presentation, lecture, seminar, study day, book, or paper never failed to inform his audience at the beginning that he was and continued to be a service user. This is critical to understanding his spirituality and his views on mental health. Not only does the service user need to be central to planning services, treatments and future care plans, but also to humanise providers of services and the places where they are provided. It is only by getting inside the skin of the sufferer that so many of the qualities associated with spirituality can be understood, viz., integrity, privacy, dignity, respect, meaning, individuality, personal value, justice, trust, purpose, self-transcending love (Swinton & Pattison, 2001), vision, kindness, compassion, equality, acceptance, and a sense of the other.

Understanding the human situation from within is a central feature of the Christian faith as well as other faith traditions. Only by becoming human could the Creator identify fully with His creation. It was St. Irenaeus who wrote that: *'Christ became man, so that man could become divine'*. This picks up another theme in Christian and other faiths' theology that each person is made in the image of God and each is called to enjoy a special relationship with God. The uniqueness and sacredness of being human is a core belief in the Christian tradition and is increasingly becoming intrinsic to spirituality. When spirituality informs practice in the health service, this understanding of the uniqueness of each individual person will ensure that the service user remains central to the process.

The history of mental health legislation

Of the four categories of Peter's work, the one which applies to me most is mental health, as a glance at my biography shows (see p4). Let me then trace the history of mental health legislation in order to show how the patient has moved from the periphery to the centre, and from patient to service user. The practice of detaining people with mental health problems under the law only began in the middle of the 19th century, a little over 160 years ago. Until then 'lunatics', as they were known, frequented the workhouse and private mental hospitals. Legislation became obligatory with the building of Broadmoor Hospital, which housed those certified as 'criminally insane'. In 1845 the first legislation appeared on the statute book and was to remain there with some revisions until 1959. Lunatics, idiots and cretins (later subnormals, later the mentally handicapped and later still, people with learning disabilities) could be certified by a magistrate and detained in a lunatic asylum. The law provided custodial care for the patient. A vigorous building programme began and some say that the Victorians devoted more resources to the care of the 'mentally ill' than any era before or since. Every city and every county was legally obliged to provide a hospital in which people could be detained. The hospitals were encircled by a wall with a sentry on duty at the main gate and all the wards were locked, with men physically segregated from women. They were built in the countryside, away from centres of population and usually approached by an avenue of trees. There was always a bend in the road to the hospital so that people outside could not see the 'inmates' and they, in turn, could not see or communicate with those outside. This gave rise to the expression 'round the bend', one of many pejorative terms used for those with mental health problems. Staff were recruited from the military and called attendants. Care was basic, physical (restraining chairs and cold water baths) and involuntary. Because people were detained by law (out of sight and out of mind), the legislation provided for 'commissioners in lunacy' to visit regularly and to oversee the care and treatment provided. Their reports are extant and make fascinating reading, and commissioners continued until the 1930s.

In the early years of the 20th century the distinction between mental illness and learning disability was recognised in law and, as a consequence, special hospital units were built, which were called colonies for the subnormal. Essentially what was being provided was once again custodial care, which acted as a protection for the general public. Huge social changes occurred between 1845 and 1959 when the government passed new mental health legislation. The changes in society were such that the world would never be the same again.

There were two world wars. After the first, men returned from the trenches with what today would be diagnosed as post-traumatic stress disorder and a range of other mental health problems, such as depression. At the same time, therapeutic techniques such as psychoanalysis were being pioneered by Freud and his disciples, which focused on the individual. By the time of the Second World War, there had been enormous developments in medication, particularly the major tranquilisers and, when soldiers returned, Wilfred Bion developed his group work, which has now become axiomatic in most areas of human interaction. It was Bion who identified in every group of eight or more, a leader, an observer and dynamics like 'fight/flight', denial of the task and rationalisation of demands placed upon the group.

All these changes and developments led to new mental health law. It is important, however, to recognise that changes in legislation usually follow social and scientific innovations, rather than precede them. With the new treatments available, the 1959 Mental Health Act focused on treatment with the result that the doors of the asylums were opened, the perimeter walls taken down (in the hospital where I worked, ironically by the patients themselves) and the general public were invited to go 'round the bend'. It was decided that the commissioners were not needed because treatment was the responsibility of the health professionals whom, it was thought, could be trusted with the care of those with mental health problems.

The new act remained on the statute book for 24 years. In that time there was more social upheaval. It was the age of the Beatles, Carnaby Street and

Flower Power. There were people experimenting with drugs and new styles of relationships. As Dr Cheryl Hunt says:

'I am reminded of the title of one of Bob Dylan's most well-known songs, 'The Times They are a-Changin''! [Released by Colombia Records in 1964]. This song captured the essence of the social and political upheaval that characterised the 1960s but it also seems particularly apt in the context of upheavals, especially those relating to spirituality and religion, that may come to define our present times.' (Hunt, 2013)

At the same time it became clear that health professionals could not be trusted with the care of those with mental health problems. Sadly, there were a number of public enquiries into the abuse by staff of patients in their care. Allied to these revelations was an increasing emphasis on the individual and individual rights, which would become enshrined in human rights legislation. All of this indicated the need for new legislation, which reached the statute book in 1983. The new Mental Health Act focused on the individual and individual rights. Because of this, the commissioners (Mental Health Act commissioners) were reintroduced to safeguard both individuals and their rights. They have a visitorial and inspectorial function, reporting to Parliament every year. In the latest report from the Care Quality Commission the detention figures in 2011/12 record that commissioners visited 1,546 wards where patients (note the change in nomenclature) were detained under the Act, met in private with 4,569 detained patients, and this is by no means the total of patients detained during that time (CQC, 2013, p4).

After 140 years of mental health legislation the emphasis is **at last** on the person and their needs. This is probably best illustrated by the introduction of 'consent to treatment' (Section 58, which contains a very rich definition of consent) and the obligation to provide aftercare (Section 117) – all of which warmed Peter's heart, though, for him, did not go far enough. Consent began a process of involving the service user in a discussion about their individual treatment. That discussion continues today, as we shall see.

Detaining someone under the Mental Health Act (1983; 2007) is a very big step to take. The only other way a person's liberty can be removed is if a person is arrested by the police or is an illegal immigrant. For this reason, in 1983 the role of the approved social worker was introduced. Two doctors *recommend* detention and the ASW *applies* for detention. After the Mental Health Act was amended in 2007, the ASW was replaced by the approved mental health professional in order to extend the role to other disciplines (DH, 2008). The AMHP is under a statutory obligation to operate according to the principle of *least restriction*, which in 2007 became the second general guiding principle when detention under the Act is being considered. Detention of a person under the Mental Health Act (1983; 2007) is, and always should be, a last resort.

At the turn of the 21st century, there was pressure from the then Labour government to introduce new legislation where the concentration was on public safety and the administration of the detention process. However, the Mental Health Alliance and the Royal Colleges put up a strong defence for amendments to the current legislation, which is patient-focused and not, they argued, 'half bad'. What was needed were amendments to the current Act to make it community- rather than hospital-based. Surprisingly, the Government listened and the amended legislation became law in 2007.

Rates of detention are available from the statistics department of the NHS and, since 1983, from the biennial reports of the Mental Health Act Commission (MHAC). When the MHAC was incorporated into the Care Quality Commission in 2009, figures were made available on an annual basis from the Commission. What these rates indicate is that, since the 80s, there has been a two-thirds shift in the location of people with mental health problems.

In 1985 the number of beds for people with mental health problems was approximately 140,000. Interestingly, these accounted for two-thirds of the total NHS beds. In 2009/10 when the Care Quality Commission began its work, this number had fallen to around 30,000. Unless there are significantly less people with mental health problems, the question arises about where people with mental health problems **are** located.

There are only two places viz. the community and the criminal justice system. Significantly, many general practitioners confirm this two-thirds shift from hospital to community. Understandably, one reason why rates of detention have increased from 1985 to 2010 is that fewer hospital beds are available. This is not the only reason for the increase in detention rates, which interestingly are higher in London than the rest of the country. To do justice to these phenomena really deserves a chapter of its own. Figures from the prison service also indicate a rise during this period. In 1985 the prison population was around 30,000 and today is nearly 90,000. It is also known from Home Office statistics that many of these people have mental health problems.

A generally accepted figure today is that one in four people will require treatment for a mental health problem at some stage in their life. When I asked Peter about this he thought that it was nearer one in one! Even with a smaller inpatient population (one reason for the increase in detention rates ie. the illness has to be more severe), great care has to be taken in how the Mental Health Act is applied.

We have already noted that, to protect patients from unnecessary detention, sectioning someone is always a last resort. A good example of the care that is required when using the legislation is the use of Section 5.2. This section enables hospital staff to detain a person who is already an inpatient for a maximum of 72 hours until a full assessment can be made and treatment begun, if required. If it is over used, the hospital will quickly gain a reputation for admitting people voluntarily and then detaining them. If it is under used, then people may leave the hospital who require treatment they may have refused. It is a delicate balance.

The legal journey from long-term custodial care to open wards and community care has taken from 1845 to 2007 (162 years) and now, hopefully, the service user is central to planning services, deciding on appropriate treatment and promoting preventative measures. This is central to Peter's work and this is the *clue* to his thinking.

Let us now turn to the resources needed if there is to be a seamless service across the whole country. At the moment the provision is patchy; some would say a 'postcode lottery' and this must be addressed as a matter of urgency. Historically, resources have been driven by the acute sector and people with mental health problems have suffered; they are at the human rather than the high tech end of the spectrum and mental health has often been described as a Cinderella service. The emphasis in acute care is on rapid intervention, short stay and home care, which does not fit well in the world of mental health where the need is for person-centred individual and group therapies, which are time consuming. I have always thought that intrinsic to any successful mental health service, is the provision of time and space. Surveys on the treatments patients prefer indicate a desire for the 'talking therapies', not least because they help to rebuild confidence and well-being.

Resources are also needed to combat prejudice and stigma (especially multi-stigma) experienced by people with mental health problems in order to avoid isolation and abandonment. The Tesco and Asda moguls and other outlets have much still to learn about stigma when, on 26th September 2013, after representation from mental health charities, they agreed to withdraw offensive 'mental health patient' Halloween dressing-up outfits from sale. Significantly, it is Pete Seeger who wrote in the song 'Where Have All the Flowers Gone?' the refrain *'When will they ever learn?'* (Seeger, 1955). The people affected are so often the most vulnerable and isolated people in society. Consedine writes this as he makes the link with spirituality (2002, p45): *'What makes for a holistic spirituality is the recognition that we are all interdependent, that we need to see the divine spark in one another and respect that, and that we need to specifically protect the most vulnerable, the poorest and the most powerless'.*

It is essential that *the service user is central to a rich provision of services and education programmes* to help change the culture of 'out of sight, out of mind'. This is something that the NIMHE/CSIP programme was developing before it was withdrawn. The Care Quality Commission is to be commended for including experts by experience in its visits. Most welcome is the initiative 'No Health Without Mental Health'. In 2011, the Government stated its commitment to parity of esteem between mental and physical services in its mental health strategy (CQC, 2013). More recently, at the 2013 Labour Party Conference Ed Miliband said that a Labour government would ensure that mental health is not an *afterthought*.

Care and support in the home may well be the best way forward for someone recovering from surgery. Home care, however, must not be allowed to influence the provision of good community-based mental health services. People with mental health problems will not flourish by being isolated in a small flat with little or no social contact. Another contributor to this book, Antony Sheehan, reminds us that a person with mental health problems needs:

- a job

- a roof over their head

- a date at the weekend.

Finally, let us look at the importance of spirituality about which Peter was so passionate. It speaks directly, unequivocally and determinedly to the centrality of the service user, quite simply because it undergirds the values required for a comprehensive mental health service. A graphic way of considering the role of spirituality is to compare the Guiding Principles (DH, 2008, chapters 1.2–1.6) set out in the Code of Practice for the amended Mental Health Act with the qualities intrinsic to spirituality.

Table 1.1: Code of spirituality	
The Code of Practice	**Spirituality**
Purpose	Purpose, meaning, vision
Least restriction	Justice, freedom
Respect	The sacredness of each person Dignity Respect
Participation	Social responsibility Compassion Acceptance and sense of the other
Effectiveness	Integrity, kindness
Efficiency	Stewardship, trust
Equity	Equality, love

All of these qualities associated with spirituality have been developed by the National Forum for Spirituality and Mental Health for which Peter was its project lead. At the same time the British Association for the Study of Spirituality has become a focus for research and the study of spirituality. Peter often said that the primary effect of his work was that it gave permission to staff to talk about spirituality with those in their care. He also developed strong links with faith communities in the UK. Like all voluntary bodies, the role of faith communities is threefold:

- pioneer new areas of work

- fill gaps in the provision of services

- monitor existing services.

Faith communities provide places where a person with mental health problems can develop natural social contacts and a group which accepts them as they are and puts them at the centre.

By putting the service user at the centre we will begin to appreciate the gifts those with enormous suffering and disability have to offer to us. Here we will find new riches, new horizons and new insights into the role of spirituality in human affairs. Let me end with a story about the support that is offered to us.

Paul was beginning his ministry as a clergyman in a local parish church. His family, including his 14-year-old daughter Lucy, who has special needs, were with him. We made sure there was plenty of space for Lucy's wheelchair and for her to be within a few feet of her father when he was ordained. Speaking to him afterwards, I said how wonderful it was that she was able to be near him. He replied 'I could not have got through it without her'.

Listening to the stories and accompanying those with mental health problems on their journeys will take us to places we have never been before, introduce us to new experiences and open a veritable store of riches, as yet untouched.

References

Care Quality Commission (2013) Monitoring the Mental Health Act 2011/12. Available at:http://www.cqc.org.uk/sites/default/files/media/documents/cqc_mentalhealth_2011_12_main_final_web.pdf (accessed November 2013).

Consedine J (2002) Spirituality and social justice. In: M Nash and B Stewart (eds) *Spirituality and Social Care: Contributing to personal and community well-being*. London: Jessica Kingsley Publishers.

Department of Health (2008) *Code of Practice Mental Health Act 1983*.Available at: http://www.lbhf.gov.uk/Images/Code%20of%20practice%201983%20rev%202008%20dh_087073%5B1%5D_tcm21-145032.pdf (accessed November 2013). Chapter 4.29.

Hunt C (2013) Editorial. *Journal for the Study of Spirituality* **3** (1) 3–7.

Swinton J & Pattison S (2001) Come all ye faithful. *Health Service Journal* **111** (5786) 24–25.

Irenaeus c.130-200 Primary 1

Seeger P (1955) Where Have All the Flowers Gone? Columbia Records.

Chapter 2: The running group

Qaisra Khan

'Deep peace of the running wave to you,
Deep peace of the flowing air to you,
Deep peace of the quiet earth to you,
Deep peace of the shining star to you,
Deep peace of the infinite peace to you.'

A Celtic blessing

It was not long after I started working as a spiritual and cultural care co-ordinator at Oxleas NHS Foundation Trust that I met Peter Gilbert at a conference. His enthusiasm for mental health, spirituality and support was invaluable during the years I worked at the Trust, and since.

Oxleas NHS Foundation Trust became a pilot within the mental health and spirituality project led by Peter. There was, therefore, an open invitation to retreats, conferences and seminars where we could share and develop ideas with others. His broad umbrella presentations about, for instance, the running group were not only uplifting but gave pause and helped in promoting the work to others. Peter often spoke about his running group as a space where people came together for a particular reason but shared their common humanity along the way. In some ways this also represented his peaceful energy and it enabled the work to develop from small steps to a running pace. It also recalls the way he would welcome you to a gathering.

As this book is a tribute to Peter's contribution to the work around mental health, spirituality and the bringing together of diverse faith perspectives, it seems appropriate to begin with a blessing from the Celtic tradition. I am particularly reminded of the blessing as I am currently working at Bishop's House on the island of Iona, which is an ecumenical community and one of the birthplaces of northern Christianity. The blessing also recalls the running group and how amongst the frenetic energy of something as dynamic as waves or running you can have peace.

Developing a connection with the Divine

Spirituality, to me, is about developing a connection to the Divine, the infinitely compassionate and merciful. This connection is helped by the signs of the universe enfolding around us. The best way to describe this is in reference to a Sikh wedding I attended where the couple walked around the Guru Granth Sahib, the holy book and guide/teacher around which their life would revolve. As the woman walked around the holy book, her brothers touched and guided her shoulders to remind her that they would always be there for her. In much the same way, the light from the sun and the changing phases of the moon give us a gentle reminder and opportunity to re-connect to our Divine and ultimate protector.

The phases of the moon guide the Islamic calendar as each month starts with a new moon. Ramadan is the ninth month and provides us with, perhaps, the greatest opportunity to reconnect with the Divine and reflect on life: a kind of retreat where you change the pattern of your life by fasting during daylight hours and reading the Qu'ran, the word of God, which was first revealed during this month. In addition to Taraweeh prayers when mosques are filled with worshippers wishing to listen to the recitation of the word of God, there are some who will disrupt their normal routine further by going into seclusion (I'tikaf), an opportunity for serious reflection and worship.

Sunset is the most dramatic daily reminder of God's presence because it is the time of the fourth formal prayer required of Muslims and the one where the opportunity to reconnect needs to be answered almost immediately because, traditionally, it does not last long: it is a great sight indeed to see people running to answer that particular call to prayer. Sunset is also the ending of the day when you are hoping that you have done what you need to do before going to sleep, which is a surrender and therefore can be a reminder of our own mortality.

Lord it is night

The night is for stillness.
Let us be still in the presence of God.

It is night after a long day.
What has been done has been done;
What has not been done has not been done;
Let it be.

The night is dark.
Let our fears
Of the darkness of the world
And of our own lives rest in you.

The night is quiet.
Let the quietness
Of our peace enfold us,
All dear to us,
And all who have no peace.

The night heralds the dawn.
Let us look expectantly
To a new day,
New possibilities.
In your name we pray.

Amen

This copyright material is taken from *A New Zealand Prayer Book: He Karakia Mihinare O Aotearoa* and is used with permission.

This connection to the rhythms of nature is not particular to one community and has been referred to by others. For instance, Noel Dermot O'Donoghue in *The Mountain Behind the Mountain: Aspects of the Celtic tradition* (2000) refers to '*a unity with nature*'. He also talks of '*a sense of human immortality, a sense that we human beings come from afar and return to that region*' and '*I can breathe freely only in the atmosphere of immortal spirit and the final transformation of nature and all that is within my own living, breathing, vulnerable human substance*' and '*The Christian message of new life and eternal salvation is not a bolt from the blue but a sunrise that takes its colours from earth and sky and sea.*'

There is a Sufi meditation technique on the first pillar of Islam, which is 'there is no God but God'. It requires us to breathe out as we form the words 'there is no God' and pause a moment before breathing in and declaring 'but God!' This meditation, prayer or reflection can be symbolic of any journey in life: that is, the darkest hour is just before the dawn. Those who have cause to use mental health services may have lost family, friends and their sense of self, so it is important to pause within a supportive environment to enable them to decide for themselves what they wish to breathe in. It is important to remember and value wherever an individual's spiritual journey is along the spectrum: a bit like the running group.

The running group is referred elsewhere in this book because of its importance to Peter and his stories, but the analogy can be applied to other situations where people come together for a common purpose: it may be a trek to the Himalayas or a journey to St. Colomba's Bay in Iona; chess, crochet or a reading group. It may even be a team of people working together to prepare a house to welcome guests as we are doing at Bishop's House, Iona. In the words of the warden, Toben Lewis: *'Working and living together in community can present many challenges; adding an ongoing rotation of volunteers to this can present even more. It can feel, at times, like we are in a constant state of training. Every time we get our staff trained up and into the rhythm of life here, one of them leaves at the end of their time with us and we start from scratch with a new person. Just as we start to really get to know someone, and really appreciate their company, their time ends and we meet someone new. But the benefits outweigh these challenges. Each volunteer brings a different perspective. We are constantly seeing things with new eyes, and learning from each person that comes to work with us. Something as simple as a 'Why do we…' question can change our process when we realise there is no rhyme or reason why we do something a certain way. Watching someone else work in the kitchen allows us to learn new techniques, new flavours. Our season goes from the beginning of March to the end of October, occasionally beyond that. By the time September rolls around we are beginning to show wear around the edges. We are beginning to tire. But in comes another fresh volunteer (or two) with energy and enthusiasm for the house, for the island, for what we can and do provide our guests. Their liveliness is infectious. The excitement of our volunteers helps to reinvigorate us, as well; and it makes for a better quality of stay for our guests when all of the staff are here for a purpose and are pleased to be here.'*

Spiritual dimensions to support and treatment

The key point is that people come together, pause, be open, and not push an agenda. We will eventually and almost inevitably begin to trust ourselves and others so we can start to share in other ways. As the fastest and fittest in the group start looking out for and helping the strugglers in the back or those who are too afraid to even start, companionship and mutual support build up. The fastest may also realise that by reading, for instance, too quickly they missed the full impact of a particular passage or poem. This breathing and pausing has parallels with mindfulness, a practice that has been of increasing benefit in mental health services. Over recent years, in fact, there has been increasing interest in treatments that include the spiritual dimension. In addition to established 12-step programmes for alcohol and substance misuse, new approaches such as mindfulness-based cognitive therapy for the treatment of stress, anxiety and depression (MBCT) and compassion-focused therapy are now being actively researched and supported; nor is this interest limited to health services.

It is important to bear in mind that people with mental health problems have said that they want:
■ to feel that they belong, are valued and trusted

■ to be treated with dignity and respect

■ to feel safe and secure

■ the chance to make sense of their life, including illness and loss

■ meaningful activity such as creative art, work or enjoying nature

■ time to express feelings to members of staff

■ permission/support to develop their relationship with God or the Absolute. (RCPsych, 2013)

We can do this by ensuring we listen effectively, take note of the whole person and not make assumptions. You may then want to ask gentle questions that will enable a person to reveal their main spiritual concerns, what sustains them and keeps them going in difficult times. Whether they feel loved or have a sense of belonging.

These questions could include what gives you hope, strength and support. What is your understanding of God? It has also proved useful to ask how an individual's faith helps them to connect, be active, learn something new, give, and be curious because research has shown these are helpful in maintaining good mental health (New Economics, 2014).

There are other approaches, such as person-centred planning and the recovery model, which are focused on helping an individual learn about themselves and to make choices. The Royal College of Psychiatrists has stated, however, that *'a gentle, unhurried approach works best – at its best, exploring spiritual issues can be therapeutic in itself'* and *'Spiritual practices can help us to develop the better parts of ourselves. They can help us to become more creative, patient, persistent, honest, kind, compassionate, wise, calm, hopeful and joyful'* (RCPsych, 2013).

Spiritual skills include key skills for living, such as:
■ being able to stay focused in the present, to be alert, unhurried and attentive

■ being able to rest, relax and create a still, peaceful state of mind

■ being able to be with someone who is suffering, while still being hopeful

■ learning better judgement, for example about when to speak or act, and when to remain silent or do nothing

- learning how to give without feeling drained

- being able to grieve and let go.

Spirituality emphasises our connections to other people and the world, which creates the idea of 'reciprocity': that is if you help another person, you help yourself.

References

New Economics Foundation (2014) *Five Ways to Well-being* [online]. Available at: http://www. neweconomics.org/projects/entry/five-ways-to-well-being (accessed January 2014).

O'Donoghue N (2000) *The Mountain Behind the Mountain: Aspects of the Celtic tradition*. Edinburgh: T & T Clark.

Royal College of Psychiatrists (2013) *Spirituality and Mental Health* [online]. Available at: http://www. rcpsych.ac.uk/expertadvice/treatments/spirituality.aspx (accessed November 2013).

The Anglican Church in Aotearoa (1988) *A New Zealand Prayer Book: He Karakia Mihinare O Aotearoa*. Available at: http://anglicanprayerbook.org.nz/contents.htm (accessed January 2014).

Further resources

BBC religion and ethics: http://www.bbc.co.uk/religion/religions/islam/

The Iona community: http://iona.org.uk/about-us/history/

The Threshold Society: http://sufism.org/

Chapter 3: Breathing out – breathing in

John Swinton

It is with great pleasure tinged with much sadness, that I offer a small contribution to this important volume dedicated to someone who has been inspirational for many and who has opened up avenues for caring that have brought blessing and healing to countless people. In this chapter I simply want to reflect on some aspects of Peter Gilbert's approach to spirituality and to offer some thoughts on the significance of his contribution to what is a vital ongoing conversation within health and social care.

Breathing in and breathing out

Peter loved running. He began running as part of his rehabilitation after a deep, powerful and life-changing experience of depression. For Peter *running was healing*. As he puts it:

'It's something about getting out in the open air, and about friendships with people… Psychologists would probably say it is about flow, and they are probably right – you get into a rhythm when you're running with others. You're sort of connected with nature, perhaps with God.' (Gilbert, 2009)

This simple statement about the spiritual dimension of running highlights some vital aspects of Peter's understanding of the nature and function of spirituality. While having spiritual roots within the Roman Catholic Church, Peter's spirituality was broad, ecumenical, compassionate and above all else, inclusive. In his view, spirituality was about healing, relationships, finding meaning, rhythm and harmony in life; connection to community, connection to the world, and for some, connection to God. Peter's love of running functions as an active, flexible metaphor for his way of understanding spirituality. As he found his rhythm in the pounding of his feet on pavement and tarmac, so he discovered an inner tempo; a deep spiritual cadence that allowed him not only to find inner healing, but also to realise that the cadence of his experience was mirrored in a multitude of valuable lives of people who had lost the steadiness and pace in their lives. Spirituality is a way of re-anchoring lives that are drifting, or have already drifted, into deep experiences of meaninglessness and dehumanisation. In an interesting and ultimately mysterious way, Peter's depression became the gateway through which he was able to enter into the world of spirituality and discover its healing potential for his life and by implication, for the lives of many people experiencing mental health issues. My point is not that depression is mystical and always meaningful. Sometimes it can be quite the opposite: dark, lonely, apophatic and meaningless. I simply want to highlight the way in which the refocusing of Peter's vision that emerged from his experience of depression helped him to reframe mental health, and to recognise that there was a deep omission of the spiritual from the ways that mental health care was, and sadly sometimes still is, conceptualised and delivered.

The art of breathing

At the heart of the practice of running is the art of breathing. If you don't breathe properly you won't run very far! Breathing, like many of our core experiences, is something that we simply take for granted and rarely reflect on. It is just always there. We seldom stand back and argue about what breathing is or whether it actually exists! A runner, however, has no choice. She needs to reflect carefully on the movement of her breathing, synchronising her inhaling and exhaling with the pounding of her feet; in harmony she shifts her breathing into line with the movements of her body. If she gets that synchronisation right, she can run for miles. If she gets it wrong she becomes exhausted and has to stop and reassess. Breathing is central to all of our activities. If we only breathe in or only breathe out; if our breathing is sporadic and unpredictable, then we will fall over and we may even die. But if we breathe in and out, then we will live well and hopefully we will flourish.

For Peter, spirituality is like breathing. We may not notice it, but it is in fact central to the happiness, joy and sadness that we experience in our lives. Spirituality in a real sense echoes the rhythm of breathing in and breathing out; of finding life and holding it in balance irrespective of our circumstances. Peter pushed us to reflect on the inward and outward movement of spirituality with regard to our understanding of individuals, services, service provision, service users and those who seek to offer and receive care and support in the midst of the dark and often dry experience of mental illness. In this way the art of running could be seen as central for Peter's understanding of spirituality and the goals of care. Breath only does its job when it effectively fills the whole body with oxygen. Service provision only does its job and achieves its goals if it reaches every dimension of the experience of service users and service providers. Spirituality is like breath for service users and service providers. Without it, understanding care and support can only be partial. Without it, service provision can never be inspirational, but is doomed to be both dispirited and dispiriting. That crucial observation was central to Peter's work and his vocation; his calling to re-open the eyes of those who have become blind to fundamental human truths and needs. The rhythm, the pace, the perseverance, the need for services to breathe properly in order that the body of care can remain fully oxygenated and energised were precisely the facets of spirituality that Peter, I suspect, learned from running, and which he captured so well in his writings and in his life.

Breathing in: spirituality

Peter's work is marked with a sense of deep practical wisdom and insight that is warm and accessible but at the same time incisive and insightful. Take for example, his basic observation about the frequency of spiritual language in our day-to-day conversations:

'You can usually tell the importance of a concept by the amount that words related to it crop up in everyday speech. We often hear people talking about someone inspiring them; and perhaps this is somebody they work with (somebody using or somebody providing a service), or perhaps an historical figure from a political, social and healthcare, religious, sporting, or military dimension. We also find ourselves catching our breath at a particularly gorgeous sunset; a mountain pass; a seascape; and declaring that it is inspirational. When services fail, those who use services; frontline staff, managers, inspectors, may often declare that someone needs to breathe some new life into this service.' (Gilbert, 2006)

This is an important insight. Spiritual experiences cause us to stop and draw breath. We find ourselves in awe in the presence of God, nature, sunsets and sometimes in the presence of people. While rock stars might make some people breathless, the mention of someone like Nelson Mandela, Martin Luther King, Emily Pankhurst or Gandhi, causes us to inhale in wonder as we breathe in their glorious moments. In the midst of a culture that claims to have moved on from spiritual things, when it comes to expressing those things that are deepest and most important to us, it is precisely this 'forgotten' language that we implicitly and explicitly fall into. I was fascinated and a little amused to hear Richard Dawkins recently challenge Christians by saying that they don't even know the titles of the books in their holy scriptures. The interviewer went on to ask him to name the full title of Darwin's *Origins of the Species* (1859). Dawkins squirmed around for a bit, exclaimed 'Oh God!' and then admitted that he had forgotten the full title (Radio 4, 2012). Even the most outspoken anti-spiritualists slide into spiritual language when put under pressure! It's something primal, but it can be beautiful.

Peter was right; the language of the spiritual is all around us. Within the Abrahamic religious traditions the term 'spirit' has profound meaning. In Hebrew the word *'nephesh'* means both breath and spirit. God breathes God's spirit into the dust and forms the first human being. Through breath, human beings were made alive. By breathing in God's *nephesh*, God's spirit, life was shared. Without the spirit of God there is nothing. But with the inspiration of God towards human beings, life becomes a possibility. In classical times 'spiritus' also meant inspiration, denoting those invisible, but real qualities, which shape the life of a person or a community, such as love, courage, peace or truth. To be spiritual in this sense is to be fully human.

But you don't have to be a religious person to recognise the power of the spirit and the incisiveness of the language of the spirit. We find sunsets *inspirational*; we find some people *inspiring* and *uplifting*. Experiences leave us *breathless*. Sadness and brokenness feel *dispiriting*. When we are disappointed we feel *deflated*. We search for new ways in which we can *breathe* new life into our service provision or aspects of our lives which have become *uninspiring*. We seek after *inspiration* when we want new ideas or to make radical changes; we try to approach people in the right *spirit*. The language of the spirit is all around us if we have eyes to see it; it reaches into those aspects of our lives that mundane language simply cannot capture. As we breathe in the spirit of change, so we are inspired to do new and perhaps wonderful things. This, I think is at the heart of what Peter was pushing for in terms of creating a context for a change of heart with regard to leadership and current service provision (Gilbert, 2005). Focusing on the spirit is nothing more, and nothing less, than remembering the depths of our humanness, or as Peter has put it: *'It's humanity, stoopid!'* (Gilbert, 2005). His point is not flippant; it's ironic. How could so many of us miss this point!?

Peter was a humanist in the best sense of the word ie. he cared deeply for human beings: *'As somebody who has worked as a practitioner and manager in a range of environments and services with all user groups, it strikes me more and more that failures in our human service systems are based on a tragic failure to recognise each other's common humanity, and also the incredible unique qualities of each individual.'* (Gilbert, 2006)

It is this basic lack of an ability to notice what seems to be remarkably obvious that sits at the heart of Peter's passion for a reclamation of the spiritual dimension of care, and sometimes his anger towards those who seem determined not to recognise its importance. As he puts it: *'I am increasingly impatient with professionals who claim that their professionalism is such, that they cannot display any human emotions, or declare human weakness, or uncertainty. I am equally impatient with members of the public who see humanity as a failure and not a strength; and with those service users who find it easier to place professionals into a professional ghetto. Increasingly, the leadership of services seems to be about the "bland leading the bland" ... where poor practice isn't challenged, and the only thing people are interested in is the tick box of performance targets, so that bad practice is allowed to wait until "the inspector calls" and it's all too late for the people who suffer!'* (Gilbert, 2006)

'The bland leading the bland.' What a fascinating phrase. Some may see the re-introduction of spirituality and its accompanying humanist values (again, I don't mean this in terms of the ideological understanding of humanism, but as a perspective on the world that truly values human beings for who they are), as meaningless; some kind of icing on the cake. Peter's perspective was that they are core, fundamental both to those who provide services and those who receive them. If we have forgotten the centrality of humanness, then what do we have left? What is required is that we all slow down, back off a little and breathe in. If human services are to be genuinely humane and truly person-centred, then the last thing that we should be doing is forgetting about the spirit, or deliberately overlooking it because of some ideological principles that enable us to pretend that we are objective and 'value free' when we approach those whom we seek to offer care and support to. Spirituality provided Peter with a powerful lever with which he could open up some obvious wounds, questions and blind spots within contemporary service provision (and the experience of those receiving such provision), in ways that return us to the centrality of personhood, the mystery of human experience and the beauty of human persons.

In this sense, Peter could be described as a radical humanist; that is, he was someone who pushed us to explore the roots of our humanness and to regain and re-collect certain aspects of being human that current assumptions about service provision have often occluded or even deliberately tried to eradicate. So Peter called us to breathe in; to reflect on how life looks when we inspire one another and attend with care and interest to those aspects of our lives which are, in fact, the most important. He helped us to pay attention to the right things. Iain McGilchrist notes the importance of paying attention to the right things: *'The nature of the attention we choose to pay alters the nature of the world we experience, and governs what it is we will find. This in turn governs the type of attention we deem it appropriate to pay. Before long we are locked into a certain vision of the world, as we become more and more sure of what it is we see. To a man with a hammer everything begins to look like a nail. And some beautiful research demonstrates that what we do not expect, we just do not see.'* (Rowson & McGilchrist, 2013)

Peter helped us to pay attention to the world in the right ways. It may well be that we see what we expect to see, which is precisely why we need inspirational guides to help us refocus our vision on those things that are right and true. That is the prophetic challenge that Peter took up and offered to us in his writings and in his life: to begin to see the world of care properly. In a world where the language games of technology tend to sing their songs at a volume that drives out other melodies, Peter's work offers us a new, rhythmic and gentle yet piercing tune that cuts through the excess noise offering healing and new possibilities.

Breathing out: friendship, community and empathic ignorance

The outward, exhaling movement of the spirit is aimed at facilitating fundamental change within individuals and within systems. If what I have said thus far is the case, it is clear that in Peter's perspective, spirituality was not an inner, peaceful sanctuary, cut off from the dirt and grittiness of politics and institutional tensions. Like the art of running, it has a goal that is simultaneously internal and outward facing. The inward dimension is contemplative and emerges from the search for meaning, purpose, hope, value and God. Here the inwards breath brings healing and a new frame in which to look at life. The exhaling dynamic of the spiritual reaches outwards to *challenge* institutions and in particular those who choose to lead institutions, and to bring healing to communities that are broken or/and which have much potential for healing and the good life. Following the tragedy of 9/11, Peter clearly picked up the baton of challenge and healing as he pushed towards a better understanding and integration of religion into our understanding of society and mental health care. He perceived religious communities and the various traditions that they represented as having huge potential for enabling and facilitating mental health. Despite the secularist, atheistic rhetoric which has become so popular recently, Peter dares to suggest that, *'since the tragic events of 9/11, faith has become an important discourse in society as a whole'* (Gilbert, 2007). This is so in general, but it is no less so in terms of mental health care provision. Unlike some protagonists of spirituality in health and social care, Peter was always at home with religion: *'Spirituality is not the opposite of religion. Religious beliefs contain strong spiritual dimensions, philosophically and historically. However, spirituality can be used as a description of belief(s) that are not formed from a formal religion and are personal to the individual who holds them.'* (Gilbert, 2008)

Such openness to diversity is an inevitable consequence of his humanness and his call for a return to the things that are *really* important. In his view, the cause – ensuring better more humane care for people with mental health issues and enabling better management and leadership structures – easily overcame any worries or concerns with regard the particularity and exclusiveness of religion and religious communities. In a way that was subtle and deeply challenging he called for professionals (and indeed all people) to practise what he described as *empathic ignorance*. Empathic ignorance, if I understand him correctly, has to do with using the imaginative ability to project one's own feelings into the situation of another in order to foster deep understanding and mutual communication (empathy), without at the same time imposing upon the other by assuming that your knowledge is greater than theirs or that your truth is more truthful than other forms of truth. So, we enter into relationships with one another recognising that we bring something to the table, but that we have much more to learn from the other than we have to give. Thus if we can encourage hospitable conversations across the traditions within which each party is prepared to learn the skill of empathic ignorance, we can all learn from one another and create communities that not only care, but understand one another at a deep level. In this way the barriers that were formed by the experience of 9/11 and the subsequent fear of religion that has emerged, can be overcome and the true potential of religious communities can be utilised in ways that bring healing instead of division; love rather than hatred and brokenness. This dynamic of empathic ignorance is a key feature of Peter's work as a whole. In the 'strange' world of mental illness, chronic and highly damaging stereotypes and false beliefs can destroy any possibility of communication between those deemed 'ill' and those who consider themselves to be 'well'. However, when the 'ill' and the 'well' learn to empathise with ignorance, we very quickly discover that we are not different and that we are bound together in a shared humanity within which our spirits and our spirituality are places where our bondedness is revealed carefully and gently.

So we can see that Peter's passion for inter-religious dialogue combined with his deep desire to encourage hospitable friendships within the mental health care system meant that his spirituality and the spirituality that he unceasingly shared with others in print and in life is special. It is grounded in love, focused on humanity and radical in its institutional and personal potential. For Peter, spirituality is not a concept or an idea (although I have had some fascinating conversations with him around the issue of exactly what spirituality is!); rather it is a way of being within which, together, we learn to see the world differently and in seeing the world differently, come to love one another a little more fully. I guess that is exactly what good friends do?

Conclusion

Peter was a spiritual runner, pounding the roads of that strange world that we call health and social care. The rhythm of his work and the power of his voice resound in many different areas from leadership and management to person-centred spiritual care, a legacy that many of us hold with deep respect. In this chapter I have tried to show a little of what his contribution looks like and to draw out something of what I have learned from him and something of what my friendship with him meant to me. I remember well sharing the floor with him at a Royal College of Psychiatrists AGM in Edinburgh. He began by saying: 'I am a mental health service user ... and I am quite proud of that!' The dissonance in the room was palpable. The idea that you could be a mental health service user, proud of that and indeed perhaps more fully human because of such an experience was, well, different from the normal frame of things! But I think that statement says something very important about Peter and the way he understood spirituality, life and humanness. The point is not that you may or may not have a mental health issue. The point is that you are a fully human being with deep and sometimes unspeakable needs. Before you are anything else, that is what you are. Even when you are struggling with life, you are first and foremost fully human. Spirituality is the place that reminds us of our priorities. Peter's witness to this in his work remains quite beautiful and without a price.

References

Gilbert P (2005) *Leadership: Being effective and remaining human*. London: Russell House Publishing Ltd.

Gilbert P (2006) Breathing out – breathing in. *Reaching the Spirit: Social Perspectives Network Study Day Paper 9*. Pages 11–18.

Gilbert P (2007) Engaging hearts and minds ... and the spirit. *Journal of Integrated Care* **15** (4) 20–25.

Gilbert P (2008) *Introduction to Spirituality, Religion and Mental Health: A brief evidence resource*. Available at: https://www.rcpsych.ac.uk/PDF/Gilbert%20Evidence%20Resource%20Doc.x.pdf (accessed November 2013).

Mickel A (2009) Peter Gilbert talks about spirituality in his new role at Worcester university. Available at: http://www.communitycare.co.uk/2009/02/27/peter-gilbert-talks-about-spirituality-in-his-new-role-at-worcester-university/ (accessed November 2013).

Radio 4 (2012) Richard Dawkins talks to Giles Fraser. Available at: http://www.youtube.com/watch?v=Hv2U2Xp2Nu8 (accessed November 2013).

Rowson J & McGilchrist I (2013) *Divided Brain, Divided World: Why the best part of us struggles to be heard*. Available at: http://www.thersa.org/__data/assets/pdf_file/0019/1016083/RSA-Divided-Brain-Divided-World.PDF (accessed November 2013).

Chapter 4: Recovery and spirituality: how the church and healthcare can develop more faith – in each other

Antony Sheehan

As I clicked through my slides I noticed that the man had an intent gaze, as if he was tracking me in a way that others in the room were not. Because I had spent the bulk of my career in the field of mental and behavioural health, and because I had just become president of an organisation that brings together faith and health, I gave a presentation at a conference for clergy on behavioural health topics. This participant approached me afterwards and filled in a critical piece of his own story, as a pastor, of confronting behavioural health in the church. He keenly remembered the day someone looked in his eyes, and he knew that this person saw his secret there. Each Sunday as he preached in church, his dependence on alcohol and cannabis got harder to hide. Prayer and repenting simply did not shake the monkey off his back. He lived at the heartbeat of the church, but it was not a safe place for him to admit that he had a problem that he did not entirely understand.

What this pastor did not realise was that he was far from alone. His story did not surprise me. Connections between spirituality and mental health have long intrigued me, and it is an issue that impassioned Peter Gilbert, especially when he was project lead for the UK's National Institute on Spirituality and Mental Health. While not everyone has a religious faith, Peter said that everyone has a spiritual dimension: *'If you are in the midst of a physical or emotional crisis, then, if you do have a religious faith, the idea of a divine entity expressing empathy for your condition and an interest in your recovery, is a powerful concept!'* (Gilbert, 2006, p12).

Mental and behavioural illnesses occur at the same rates in faith congregations as they do in the general population – about one in four people will require professional help at some point in their lives (Stanford, 2012). While spirituality does not automatically insulate people from these disorders, it can make an indispensable contribution to recovery. A breach in healing occurs when faith communities and healthcare systems fail to recognise that both statements are true.

Peter Gilbert used to talk about Basil Fawlty, the frazzled, caricatured hotel owner played by John Cleese in Fawlty Towers. Basil muttered to himself, 'Don't mention the war'. Peter's observation was that people using mental health services often reminded themselves, 'Don't mention God'. Everywhere Peter went, they told him: *'They dare not mention their spiritual or religious beliefs for fear of being seen as in a deteriorating mental state and having their medication increased'* (Gilbert, 2006, p14). Peter, though, recognised that if mental health providers do not take spirituality seriously, they cannot hope to keep people well, or work with them for recovery.

Fifty years ago, Granger Westberg, an American Lutheran pastor and educator, pioneered an approach that integrates faith and health. In addition to opening church-based health clinics, he conducted studies about the role of clergy – and thus churches – in mental health. Westberg underscored that 40% of all people with emotional needs approached clergy first, before seeking out a mental health professional (Westberg & Draper, 1966). More recently, the work of Matthew S. Stanford, professor of psychology and neuroscience at Baylor University, affirms the same maxim (Stanford & McAlister, 2008). According to Stanford and McAlister (2008), Americans with mental and behavioural health issues first turn to pastors and priests, not psychologists. This fact has not changed in the decades between Westberg and Stanford. Its persistence challenges both healthcare systems and churches to plumb the benefits of building partnerships rather than separating from each other.

All major faith systems have core teachings that affect their views of mental health. Buddhism, for example, values 'mindfulness' even in times of illness and seeks meaning in suffering. The Jewish faith, which shares considerable sacred texts with Christianity, has never separated the mind from the body.

How are faith communities responding to the opportunity to come alongside people living with mental illness themselves or in their families? My own work has brought me to a point of specifically asking this question about Christian churches.

In the lineage of Westberg, the Church Health Center in Memphis, Tennessee, offers a model of helping churches engage with health. Through partnership with churches, the Church Health Center seeks to reclaim the biblical commitment to healing and to help people not only medically, but also by supporting them to have more love and joy in their lives and be closer to God – in other words, recognise the power of spirituality for health. This approach is central to the Church Health Center's recovery ministry, which is a growing dimension of the work. The Center supports the underserved in a city that has significant social need and limited resources for those with mental health problems.

Shame, stigma, and missed opportunity

We might think that faith communities would naturally bring spirituality to the table to address issues of healing because they are inclusive social structures with a web of relationships and have theological underpinnings for their priorities. This is not always the case. Stanford's work, looking particularly at Christian churches, goes beyond noting that people turn to the church and considers how people describe their interactions when they seek help for a mental or behavioural illness. Sadly, about 30% report encounters that work against the pursuit of health (Stanford, 2012). The largest self-description of their experiences suggest that churches either did not want to be involved with mental illness or did not sustain their support, leaving people feeling abandoned. Others were told that their disorders resulted from demonic activity, lack of faith, or personal sin (Stanford, 2012). Stanford references several studies that suggest *an initial negative interaction with the local church may cause hurting and wounded individuals to isolate themselves from a potentially beneficial support system, the religious community'* (Stanford, 2012).

In other words, churches perpetrate the same kind of stigma about mental illness as people encounter in the general culture, though the language may be baptised in the religious terminology of a particular faith tradition. That the problem is due to sin suggests a lack of righteousness. Advice to pray more suggests faithlessness. A lack of 'victory' means the person has not genuinely surrendered and repented. Somehow the afflicted are not trying hard enough or are bringing the illness on themselves. Instead of help, the ill hear a message that says, 'Get yourself together, and then come back'. The weight of the illness, compounded by the sense that it should be a secret in order to avoid public shame – inner shame happens anyway – means that people in need of healing find themselves outside the mainstream of congregational life.

Even if churches would say they do not believe this interpretation of mental illness, often they do not know what to do for or with people who struggle with emotional, mental, or behavioural health issues. One in four people already in the church at some stage in their life is affected by some condition that falls on the wide spectrum of mental and behavioural health issues, so even if churches never reach beyond their own walls, they are missing an opportunity to connect in healing ways with people already in their midst.

Jesus and mental health

What do we see in the life and ministry of Jesus that might help Christian churches respond in ways that bridge spirituality and issues of mental health more effectively?

First, we must focus on the truth that people came to Jesus for healing, and Jesus healed willingly. In just one of many passages in the gospels describing Jesus' healing work, Matthew wrote: *'So his fame spread throughout all Syria, and they brought to him all the sick, those who were afflicted with various diseases and pains, demoniacs, epileptics, and paralytics, and he cured them'* (Matthew 4:24 NRSV). Conditions, such as demon possession, are illnesses we would put in the category of mental illness today. What we see in the gospels is that mental illnesses are listed right along with health issues we think of as physical – deafness, blindness, paralysis, pain. People with mental illness came to Jesus, or others brought them, and he healed them.

The mention of demon possession causes a stumbling block for some readers of the gospel stories because it suggests a spiritual cause for destructive illness. Do demon possession and mental illness equate? If we get distracted with that inquiry, we miss the point that Jesus is interested in healing every manifestation of suffering.

Second, Jesus urged people to 'walk the talk'. In Matthew 23:3–4, Jesus says of the Pharisees, *'Do not do as they do, for they do not practise what they teach. They tie up heavy burdens, hard to bear, and lay them on the shoulders of others; but they themselves are unwilling to lift a finger to move them'*. Many of us recognise the signs of behavioural ill-health in others, and we may feel some degree of compassion. But do we help and heal? Or do we add to their burdens?

People with mental, emotional, or substance disorders often become desperate for healing. If clergy encourage them to pray more, they likely will because they are ready to try anything. When this prayer does not lead to healing, however, their misperceptions of spiritual truths confound their ability to reach out to God. Now their self-talk includes, 'God must not care enough about me to answer my prayers,' or 'I guess I'm not worthy for God to heal me'. In our care for them and encouraging their spirituality, we must be careful not to add to their burdens.

Third, Jesus consistently included people on the outskirts, the margins of society – the 'sinners', ritually unclean lepers, women and children with no standing in the social structure. What does his inclusive approach to whole-life healing ministry tell us about ours? Acceptance and welcome are at the heart of the gospel. Jesus cared for the whole person.

Fourth, we see in the gospels that Jesus had a ministry of teaching, preaching, and healing. Just as he taught in parables 'the kingdom of God is like…,' he demonstrated the kingdom when he healed. He gave people beautiful pictures of the hope and healing God wants for them.

Churches have these examples in their sacred texts. It is not difficult to see that churches, full of people who believe these teachings, can also be places that embody hope and healing for every kind of illness. Linking healthcare structures with faith communities harnesses the strengths of both.

A practical approach for churches

The Church Health Center in Memphis, Tennessee, intentionally builds on a faith foundation to translate theology into practical action. A doctor can treat a medical condition, but healthcare practitioners working in tandem with faith practitioners will be effective at not only getting through the immediate crisis, but also bringing a healing presence into a broken life. The clergy conference where I met the pastor who had struggled with alcohol and cannabis is an example of this correlation. Connecting spirituality and recovery will not look the same in every congregation, but broad categories will help both clergy and laypeople consider how to be less fearful of behavioural health and respond to the need for help in incorporating spirituality into recovery.

Recognition

One point Westberg made as far back as 1966, and others since have reiterated, is that clergy and others in the faith community know people in their real lives. They can recognise when someone is in trouble (Westberg & Draper, 1966).

Rick was a former church board member and treasurer. When his wife died after a tortuous illness, people noticed he did not come to church as often – and when he did, he was likely to be intoxicated or trembling from the effort of not drinking for the length of the service. Everyone knew he was in trouble.

Unfortunately, no one in the small congregation knew how to help. Instead they avoided Rick until he stopped attending altogether and then breathed a collective sigh of relief. This was a missed opportunity to bring healing into Rick's life not just because of his substance use disorder, but also the grief underlying it. While no one in Rick's congregation was trained for his situation, resources in the wider community might have helped. Because the people in the church understood what triggered Rick's excessive drinking, they were in a position to walk alongside him even if they themselves lacked the expertise he needed.

One tool the Church Health Center has begun using with congregations is Mental Health First Aid, a public education course from the National Council for Community Behavioral Healthcare that gives an overview of mental illness and substance use disorders in the US. Participants learn to recognise risk factors and warning signs and to take concrete action to help people in crisis. Although this is not a faith-based programme, churches are logical places to use it. Faith communities are already inclined to care for members of the congregation – like Rick – and surrounding neighborhoods. They see the benefit of a tool from healthcare professionals.

Referral

Telling people to pray more and try harder does not work for mental health recovery any more than it does for diabetes or near-sightedness. And few pastors are trained counsellors, beyond a required class or two in seminary. Every faith community would benefit from a directory of local resources. Most likely such a list already exists, and someone from the church needs only to make a few telephone calls to discover a hospital system or community resource centre ready to gladly share it. Though the list should include services available to people who may be low-income, uninsured or both, mental and behavioural illnesses strike across economic and social spectrums. Even people with adequate financial means may need support with knowing where to turn for help.

Referring people means more than handing someone a phone number. Sometimes it is enough to help them know where to go. Often, however, they need friendship in the form of help getting there or an invitation to coffee later to talk confidentially about how it went. Just as relationship helps in the recognition process, it also helps sustain a healing presence through the referral process.

Recovery

For most people the word 'recovery' connotes a substance use disorder and the reality that people who have experienced addiction remain in recovery their entire lives. Staying sober is a daily choice. People with other forms of mental illness may have a similar experience of choosing every day to pursue activities and treatments that contribute to managing their conditions. Congregations of any faith that support spirituality as part of improving wellness serve their people well.

For instance, people with mental illness often have to drop out of common activities and social settings as they heal. They may not be able to work steadily, or they may need new friends who will be sensitive to situations that are triggers for them. Churches, with their varied programmes and volunteer opportunities, can offer flexible ways for people with mental illness to participate meaningfully in the life of the faith community without demanding from them something their illness means they cannot give.

Beyond being a safe social setting, churches can be intentional about ministries that resonate with people with mental and behavioural health concerns. Faith-centered support groups for particular conditions, such as mood disorders and personality disorders, can be of enormous help. Special worship services also can be a powerful tool.

St. John's United Methodist Church in Memphis, Tennessee, launched a Friday evening service called 'The Way' that speaks to people in recovery – from any kind of illness or life trauma. Certainly many people who attend have substance use disorders, but many others also find refuge in the service. Held in the main sanctuary, The Way is led by a member of the pastoral staff who is in recovery himself. It draws people seeking spirituality and community but who may feel uncomfortable in many Sunday morning church services.

The Way also is an avenue for healthcare providers to point patients toward the benefits of spirituality in the healing process. St. John's is located across the street from the family practice clinic of Church Health Center and only two blocks from a major faith-based hospital. The proximity allows clinicians literally to walk people across the street and introduce them to the pastor who leads The Way or promise to meet them at The Way. St. John's and the Church Health Center have cultivated a thriving relationship for decades, living out the connection between faith and health that Christians see in the pages of the Bible.

Renewal

For the one-fourth of the general population affected by mental or behavioural disorders, deciding to pursue wellness is no small feat. In a culture that stigmatises mental illness, admitting you have an illness takes courage. Seeking help takes nerve. And living among a community while being transparent about an illness is pure valour.

People do not manufacture courage on their own. We all need reminders of our value to God and our place in the community not for being well, but just for being. The church offers a refresher course in the truth of God's love along with renewal of belonging and acceptance that satisfy basic human needs. In this context, we feel reinvigorated to choose to pursue wellness for another day.

Faith and health is not an 'us' versus 'them' dynamic, with an individual with mental health issues as the monkey in the middle, passed back and forth. Rather healthcare organisations and faith communities can build a relationship of mutual understanding of the strength each brings to the common goal of supporting people in greater levels of whole-life health.

Peter Gilbert put skin on his conviction that spirituality matters to mental health. He did not define the terms in religious language but in ways that ordinary people can understand and respond to. What makes us tick? What is the deepest part of humanity? What is our quest for meaning and purpose? He also shared willingly out of his own journey through a depression that required treatment. He was the 'one in four', but he embraced the humanity of his experience and sought both medical and spiritual care, recognising that in tandem they carry the power to heal.

References

Gilbert P (2006) *Breathing out – breathing in. Reaching the Spirit: Social Perspectives Network study day paper nine*. Available at: http://www.spn.org.uk/fileadmin/spn/user/*.pdf/Papers/SPN_Papers/spn_paper_9.pdf (accessed November 2013).

Stanford MS (2012) Mindful of grace: viewing mental illness through the eyes of faith. *Church Health Reader* **2** (4) 10.

Westberg G & Draper E (1966) *Community Psychiatry and the Clergyman*. Springfield, IL: Charles C. Thomas.

Stanford MS & McAlister KR (2008) Perceptions of serious mental illness in the local church. *Journal of Religion, Disability and Health* **12** (2) 144.

Resources

Mental Health First Aid: www.mentalhealthfirstaid.org

Chapter 5: Life is a mystery to be lived, not a problem to be solved: mental health as an adventure and a journey

Stephan Ball

For Peter Gilbert, spirituality was as natural as water is for fish and air is for humans – breathing in, breathing out, a favourite metaphor of his and mine; something down to earth and part of life. Similarly for me, the spiritual element is something of which I seem to have been aware all my life.

The language we use can affect the way we see things, how we shape things and how we are shaped. Describing life as a mystery to be lived rather than as a problem to be tackled, and mental health as an adventure and a journey, opens up possibilities and new ways of seeing ourselves in relation to life. This applies to health, mental health, and well-being, and in particular seeing them as not simply achieved by the prevention, diagnosis and treatment of disease, important though these are. Similarly, pain, mental distress or illness and disease are not problems to be solved but something to be lived through out of which health emerges. It changes the way we respond and how we set about shaping our lives, our relationships, our services, as well as the resources allocated and choices we make in relation to our health and mental well-being.

As part of a diploma course in psychotherapy in the 1990s I outlined my approach to therapy, and to mental health and life, by focusing on three areas that seem just as valid for me today: *a sense of identity, being; a need to belong; a search for meaning, purpose and significance in life*. I want to take these elements and explore how they relate to mental health and the role of spirituality. I will then look at the implications for today and possible avenues for further exploration and action in the future.

My inspiration for writing this chapter has been an open and enquiring approach to life and mental health, one that people like Michael Wilson in his book, *Health is for People* (1975) and which Peter, more recently, in so many of his writings and talks, also shared. Wilson affirmed for me the importance of maintaining the broadest vision for health – mental, social and spiritual as well as physical. I believe that many of Wilson's ideas are still of value today in spite of needing to update the language and emphasis for the 21st century. Wilson believed in possibilities and took various strands and explored them in ways not so dissimilar from the way Peter often did. His ideas ranged far and wide to include: health is for people; cannot be possessed, only shared; is a co-operative and collaborative effort; is interpersonal; is not competitive; involves choice and priorities; goes beyond the basic biological needs of life pointing to potential and quality in human life and relationships; does not exclude suffering; is an adventure; is a surprising gift. These ideas also embraced mental health.

Being and identity

A sense of *identity* refers to the essence of the individual, who I am as an individual, the authentic and 'real' me, my sense of self, the personal – it is my journey.

British society greatly values the individual, individual needs and choice and this is reflected in mental healthcare and policy. This is partly achieved through competition and consequently increasing fragmentation of services and partly by focusing on short-term results rather than the longer term – cure rather than prevention, public health, counselling or rehabilitation; targets and value for money rather than quality. Although not wrong in themselves, this way of doing things tends to lead to less collaboration and sharing of ideas and good practice. It also highlights a growing concern that many feel more isolated, lonely and experience increased stress and mental health problems – one in four people will experience some kind of mental health problem in their lifetime (DH, 2011), while at least one in three GP consultations are to do with mental health and many more will have a mental health component (NICE, 2011).

Health is a value word that involves choice and priorities eg. if money is spent on this disease or that surgery or medication then there will be less money for something else, such as public or preventative health or for mental health; and within mental health, money spent on hospitals means less money for treatment in the community or prevention.

Services are often geared around the individual and their needs, working with them through individualised assessments and care plans focusing on psychological therapies, medication and other treatments. By contrast, meeting social needs and providing group activities has received less priority in recent years because of a combination of change in focus and limited resources.

There is nothing wrong in itself with focusing on the individual and their needs or the choices they make. Many of the more creative and positive changes in the direction in mental health have centred on the individual, some with a spiritual dimension. Some examples include:

- the user movement having a more central role and influence on the way services are delivered and on policy, for example in being at the forefront in seeking to have their spiritual needs taken seriously (see Faulkner & Layzell, 2000; Nicholls, 2002)

- the recovery model recognises that spirituality is a vital part of recovery for many (see NIHME, 2005)

- a wide range of spiritual practices focus on the individual, such as mindfulness; meditation; yoga; being and living more in the present moment, so limiting the impact of anxious and other thoughts (see Mental Health Foundation, 2007a; Coyte, 2007a)

- assessment of an individual's spiritual and religious needs is now included in many NHS trusts' care and treatment plans for service users (eg. Moult, 2013; see also further resources)

- many NHS trusts have chaplains or small teams for cultural and faith needs who work with individuals, as well as with faith communities and staff

- psychological therapies such as cognitive behavioural therapy and other treatments; a focus on strengths, self-esteem, problem solving and developing resilience.

There is an element of health being a surprising gift, not just an achievement (Wilson, 1975, p 81), something to be cherished, nurtured, allowed to grow and flourish in a way that also includes accepting that we are all vulnerable and wounded and need to take responsibility. Is this also true of mental health? There is no doubt that this perspective raises awkward questions about fairness and why some people from birth are not allowed this gift. That relates to the sense of health and mental health as a journey and that everything, including our suffering and struggles, is included and to be lived through rather than necessarily avoided, treated or eliminated.

A need to belong

At the same time there seems to be some sort of yearning within us for being part of something, a need to *belong*, to be in relationship with other people and the environment, for community, to connect and make contact, the interpersonal. I need others to accompany me and challenge me on my journey. We are, after all, social animals albeit with our own unique identities – *ubuntu*: 'I am because we are' (from South Africa), we are human beings through our relationships. We mostly grow up in families; get educated at school and often further education. We may be involved in local faith communities and various clubs or activities, and often work or volunteer with others.

One of the changes over the latter part of the last century in Britain, and continuing into this century, has been a moving away from neighbourhood to social network or from community of place to community of interest or association (Clark, 1977). Where we spend our time and energy is increasingly through work, a faith group, or organisations or activities focused on a particular interest. It will be interesting to see what impact the use of social media and the internet has and will continue to have on both ourselves as individuals and as a community.

Most people want to be part of networks where they are recognised, accepted and valued, and where they feel they belong. This is now more likely to be through a common interest than a place and increasingly through social media.

In my experience over the years as a mental health practitioner I found that many service users, especially with severe and enduring mental health needs, developed strong social networks that would be available for social support as well as emotional and crisis support when needed and, as a consequence, often developed greater resilience. These networks grew out of meeting in day hospitals or drop-in centres, which provided safe, non-demanding spaces. Those more recently unwell with brief spells in hospital and with no similar facilities often found it harder and felt more isolated.

We need to continue to look for new opportunities to create, build and strengthen networks of support of various kinds. One recent example is the Recovery College in South London, which works with service users based on an educational model by developing and providing a range of psychological, practical and spiritual skills according to need and demand. Another example is someone who has just finished being an artist in residence at the Worcester mental health trust after 10 years and who established art and creative groups that transformed individuals' lives, enabled people to develop skills and self-confidence, and inspired people to stay connected over the years as part of a loose network.

We also need to find ways for people to connect and come together, especially where there is a mental health difficulty. One example is a GP practice in Bristol using social mirroring to map people's social networks and preferences and then to match them up with local groups such as a walking or food group for people to join and be part of. Getting people into local activities and groups and 'normalising', works for some but not all service users I have worked with, especially those with enduring mental health needs. Befriending services and local drop-ins, many established by churches and faith communities, form vital support networks for many service users. Churches and faith communities are also able to provide social contact and community involvement and engagement, partly through activities, as well as being places where people may often, but not always, feel accepted and valued (Mental Health Foundation, 2007a, p29–57). Other ways in might be through rituals or rites of passage, possibly including anniversaries, birthdays, festivals and big national sports events like the Olympics.

One of the challenges we face in Britain is the tension between the 'I' and the 'We', focusing on the individual or the community, and getting the balance right: is there too much 'I' and not enough 'We'? Increasingly I see the need and value of interdependence, which is the way most of us live and experience life, rather than independence, which has become the driving force of modern mental health services with rapid discharge rather than 'holding' people over time through ups and downs, especially those with enduring mental health needs.

Mental health services mostly focus on individual needs and less on the social and wider community resources that we all need to grow in this life; and none more so than someone with mental health issues. It is complex and involves considerable joined up thinking and collaboration of the kind Wilson refers to in *Health is for People* (1975), summarised in later reflections as *'Health is something we make together'* (Wilson, 1979, p2).

Meaning, purpose and significance

The third strand is a search for meaning and purpose, making sense of life, of pain, struggles and losses, including death; finding some purpose in existence and honouring the soul and spirituality. Linked to this is the significance a person attributes to their beliefs, values, spirituality or faith.

Psychoanalyst and holocaust survivor Viktor Frankl focused on the meaning of life, which for him was present in every moment of living and was fundamental to mental health. A quote Peter was fond of using puts it well: *'Man is not destroyed by suffering, he is destroyed by suffering without meaning'* (Frankl 1959, quoted in a 2013 talk by Peter). In mental illness, meaning and purpose may be lost so there is a need to seek, recover or remake meaning in the face of changed experiences and circumstances. This quest for meaning and making sense of what is happening can provide a source of strength, motivation and hope on life's journey at such times.

Spirituality

Spirituality is a word that has different meanings for different people at different times in different cultures. Spirituality can be described as: *'that which sustains or nurtures us'*; *'that which makes "me" me and "you" you'*; *'something that helps you make sense of your situation'* (Coyte, 2007b).

Such a definition may include: giving meaning and direction to life, motivation; a way of understanding the world and someone's place in it; belief in a higher being or a force greater than any individual; a person's religion or faith; a core part of their identity and essential humanity; a feeling of belonging or connectedness; a quest for wholeness, hope or harmony; a sense that there is more to life than material things (Mental Health Foundation, 2007b, p2)

My sense is that in our Western society spirituality most commonly refers to that which is somewhat subjective, personal and individually focused. However, it could also be argued that spirituality is both a personal and social process *'relating to ideas, concepts, attitudes and behaviours deriving from a person's or a community's interpretation of their experiences of the spirit'* (Swinton, 2001, p20). This more communal or social and relational aspect of spirituality is something that tends to be marginalised in favour of the individual. It may repay us to consider the common good, the social dimension and community in mental healthcare and support.

For me, spirituality is the thread that brings to life, connects and weaves together these three elements. It helps connect ourselves, one another, health, mental health, the environment; who we are and who we are called to be as individuals and communities with a sense of meaning and purpose our relationships with others as well as our relationship with the Other (which can be defined as all that is around us as much as supernatural entity or transcendent being).

Living learning arena

One of the ideas raised by Wilson, and one which I have found particularly intriguing over time, is the idea of the *'living learning arena'*. It has to do with the way we learn about our experience – in this case, health – in, say, a hospital or health centre/GP practice (Wilson, 1975, p91–93).

I am particularly interested to see how this could be adapted in mental health terms. For example, in psychiatric units – what do we learn about mental health and well-being from them? All too often a medical model is dominant, the doors are locked, and there is little by way of therapeutic or structured activities. They are no longer quite the places of asylum to reflect, to have space, to recover. Community mental health teams focus on time-limited support and skills-based interventions, leaving some of the areas raised earlier in doubt.

There are examples of pioneering projects that provided a window onto different possibilities from those current at the time. The prevailing ethos of the medical model, experts and specialists of the first few decades of the NHS were challenged by centres such as the Peckham Health Centre in south London in the 1930s and Ombersley Road Practice in Birmingham in the 1970s (Wilson, 1975 p92–93; Rigler, 1979).

A modern example in mental health is a project involving GP practices and other services and resources in the Sandwell area of Birmingham, an integrated primary care approach to mental health and well-being. Its aim is to use a collaborative model to find out what the needs are of the local population and to provide or support responses that enable them to take more control over their lives, build resilience, contribute to mental well-being and recovery, as well as to be able to contribute to their family and community life. This is achieved by building relationships, including with local faith communities, education, taking risks and using evidence-based research and practice amongst a wide range of creative ways. The evidence so far indicates there is less use of psychiatric hospital admission beds, people are able to stay in their local community with appropriate family and other support, in addition to other social and community benefits (NHS Confederation, 2012).

Sharing stories

Many churches and faith communities have been seeking to understand the mental health needs of individuals and offer resources, information and support in the journey of mental health, well-being and recovery, including sharing stories from survivors. There is a need for more people who have experienced mental health problems and for carers to share their stories and to have them published (see further resources).

For example, Quakers in recent years have been responding to a growing concern in this area. We have been running courses for those involved in pastoral care in our local Quaker Meetings (worship groups) to better understand and deal with issues to do with mental health and distress. People are beginning to feel more able to share their stories, their challenges, their difficulties and their joys as individuals and in Meetings when experiencing mental distress or illness. We are planning to publish some of these in 2014 (Quaker Life Network, 2014). We have also had, and plan to continue to have, various meetings to explore and share experiences, ideas, good practice and what works and what doesn't work.

This work builds on early Quaker concerns for the care of individuals with mental health problems especially through the setting up of The Retreat Hospital in York in 1796, which was based on humanity and kindness, with respect for the dignity of the individual and particular attention to their comfort. These arise out of the Quaker Way, a way of life based on the belief that there is that of God in everyone, worship centred in silent waiting, and putting faith into action especially in key areas such as equality, truth and integrity, and peace and justice.

Some ideas to explore further which recognise the individual, social and meaning or purpose dimensions of the spiritual include: adapting the model of circles of accountability where a small network of people agree to be available to a person with enduring mental illness or personality issues on a regular basis and support one another – the original model is based on work with paedophile offenders; setting up more and diverse befriending networks; a mental health helpline for people with mental health issues, similar to Silverline, which provides both an opportunity for people who are lonely or in distress to talk to someone as well as information and links to the person's local community where they can meet people and take part in activities etc. – research would be needed as to boundaries, time, resources etc.; and it may be possible to build on existing helpline services.

Conclusion

In my experience as a mental health practitioner, a friend, a volunteer, a committee member, listening and helping, or working with people with mental health difficulties over the years, their needs, hopes, aspirations and what they want are similar to everyone else according to their circumstances, personality, cultural background and so on. Mental health services have increasingly become more narrowly focused on skill-based interventions, leaving gaps for many service users in terms of social networks, work, meaningful activities, a sense of belonging and community, and of being valued. The role of spirituality in many ways can help to bridge and support these areas.

It remains to be seen whether the recent emphasis on localism (but with reduced money and resources), and the coming together of health and social care will make a difference. Like true community development working from grassroots needs and energies rather than imposed from outside, perhaps it will be service users and allied friends and supporters who help bring change about. There are many willing to listen, some to respond in various ways and some trying out innovative and different ways to express and explore this. Michael Wilson and Peter were both pioneers in different ways.

At the end of the day, it is often the simple things we need to remember most: a smile, a kind word or action, a word of encouragement or affirmation; being alongside, listening to people's stories, being willing to accompany people with mental health problems on their journey as whole people with individual, social, emotional and spiritual needs; a dose of compassion and love. People want time and space – to be really heard and 'believed in' both as an individual and as part of a community, giving a sense of belonging; to be interdependent, not necessarily independent. Fundamentally, people, with or without mental health issues, want to be loved, valued, respected and accepted. We need to rediscover this power of love to heal with compassion and kindness, something the Francis report on care in Staffordshire also highlighted. I found it increasingly difficult as a mental health practitioner within the NHS to have the time and space needed to put this into practice, though I hoped I managed to retain my sense of compassion and empathic endeavour in all I did.

Spirituality, as outlined in this chapter, seems to me to embrace a whole person approach to mental health, including the challenges and the pain; and one that offers hope and acceptance as well as love and compassion. This approach to the adventure and journey of life and mental health needs courage, compassion and comes with a cost.

References

Clark D (1977) *Basic Communities: Towards an alternative society*. London: SPCK.

Coyte ME (2007a) *Spiritual practice day by day – Conversations with those who know*. In: Coyte ME, Gilbert P & Nicholls V (Eds) (2007) *Spirituality, Values and Mental Health: Jewels for the journey* pp194–205. London: Jessica Kingsley.

Coyte ME (2007b) The service user/survivor perspective. In: P Gilbert & H Kalaga (eds) *Nurturing Hearts and Spirit: Papers from the multi-faith symposium held at Staffordshire University on 1st November 2006* pp31–38. Staffordshire: Centre for Spirituality Health, Staffordshire University.

Department of Health (2011) *No Health Without Mental Health*. London: DH.

Department of Health (2014) *Closing the Gap: Priorities for essential change in mental health*. London: DH.

Faulkner A & Layzell (2000) *Strategies for Living*. London: Mental Health Foundation.

Gilbert P (2013) *Leading with Spirit: Something inside so strong: soul-ful leadership. A talk for the National Forum for Spirituality and Mental Health*. Available at: www.mhspirituality.org.uk/resources/talks/ (accessed January 2014).

Mental Health Foundation (2007a) *Keeping the Faith: Spirituality and recovery from mental health problems*. London: Mental Health Foundation. (See especially p16 and 20–21.)

Mental Health Foundation (2007b) *Making Space for Spirituality: How to support service users*. London: Mental Health Foundation.

Moult S (2013) *A Simple Guide to Spiritual Assessment: Information for staff*. Coventry: Coventry and Warwickshire Partnership Trust.

NHS Confederation (2012) *A Primary Care Approach to Mental Health and Well-being: Case study report on Sandwell*. London: NHS Confederation

Nicholls V (2002) *Taken Seriously: The Somerset Spirituality Project*. London: Mental Health Foundation.

National Institute for Health and Care Excellence (NICE) (2011) *Greater Support for GPs to Help Diagnose Common Mental Health Disorders*. Available at: http://www.nice.org.uk/newsroom/news/GreaterSupportForGPsToHelpDiagnoseCommonMentalHealthDisorders.jsp (accessed January 2014).

NIHME (2005) *NIHME Guiding Statement on Recovery*. London: NIHME.

Quaker Life Network (2014) *The Quakers (Religious Society of Friends* [online]. Available at: www.quaker.org.uk (accessed January 2014).

Rigler M (1979) Ombersley Road. *Community* **23** (Spring) 12–13.

Swinton J (2001) *Spirituality and Mental Health Care: Rediscovering a 'forgotten' dimension*. London: Jessica Kingsley.

Wilson M (1975) *Health is for People*. London: Darton, Longman and Todd Ltd.

Wilson M (1979) The winter of materialism. *Community* **23** (Spring) 1–3.

Further reading

Spirituality and mental health and definitions of spirituality

Cornah D (2006) *The Impact of Spirituality Upon Mental Health: A review of the literature*. London: Mental Health Foundation.

Gilbert P & Parkes M (2011) *Report on the Place of Spirituality in Mental Health*. London: National Spirituality and Mental Health Forum.

Mental Health Foundation (2007) *Keeping the Faith: Spirituality and recovery from mental health problems*. London: Mental Health Foundation. (See especially pages 16 and 20–21.)

Mental Health Foundation (2007) *Making Space for Spirituality: How to support service users*. London: Mental Health Foundation.

Swinton J (2001) *Spirituality and Mental Health Care: Rediscovering a 'forgotten' dimension*. London: Jessica Kingsley.

Spiritual assessments

Culliford L & Eagger S (2009) Assessing spiritual needs. In: C Cook, A Powell & A Sims (Eds) *Spirituality and Psychiatry* Chapter 2. London: RCPsych Publications.

Eagger S & Mc Sherry W (2011) *Assessing a person's spiritual needs in a healthcare setting*. In P Gilbert (Ed) *Spirituality and Mental Health*. Chapter 10. Brighton: Pavilion Publishing.

Gilbert P & Parkes M (2011) *Report on the Place of Spirituality in Mental Health*. London: National Spirituality and Mental Health Forum.

Royal College of Psychiatrists leaflets on 'A guide to the assessment of spiritual concerns in mental healthcare', 'Mental Health and Spirituality' and 'Spirituality in psychiatry: implementing spiritual assessment' by Sarah Eagger at www.rcpsych.ac.uk.

Community and building resilience

MIND (2013) *Building Resilient Communities: Making every contact count for public mental health*. London: MIND Publications and online.

Church and faith groups and mental health

Being Alongside (formerly Association for Pastoral Care in Mental Health) at: www.beingalongside.org.uk

Catholic Church: www.mentalhealthproject.co.uk

Church of England and Mentality (2005) *Promoting Mental Health: A resource for spiritual and pastoral care*. London: Mentality and Church of England Archbishops Council.

Jewish Association For the Mentally Ill (JAMI): http://jamiuk.org/

Keeping Health in Mind: www.keepinghealthinmind.org.uk

National Spirituality and Mental Health Forum: www.mhspirituality.org.uk

Service user/survivor perspectives

Devon Partnership Trust (2009) *Beyond the Storms – Reflections on Personal Recovery in Devon: A collection of stories of personal recovery from mental illness*. Contact Jayne Clarke via jayneclarke@nhs.net.

Mental Health Foundation (1999) *The Courage to Bare Our Souls*. London: MHF.

Other groups and organisations

Art and social network for people with mental health problems in Worcester (AIMS): www.artinminds.org.uk

The Recovery College: www.swlstg-tr.nhs.uk

The Retreat (Independent non-profit making Quaker mental health hospital in York): www.theretreatyork.org.uk

Spirituality and social care

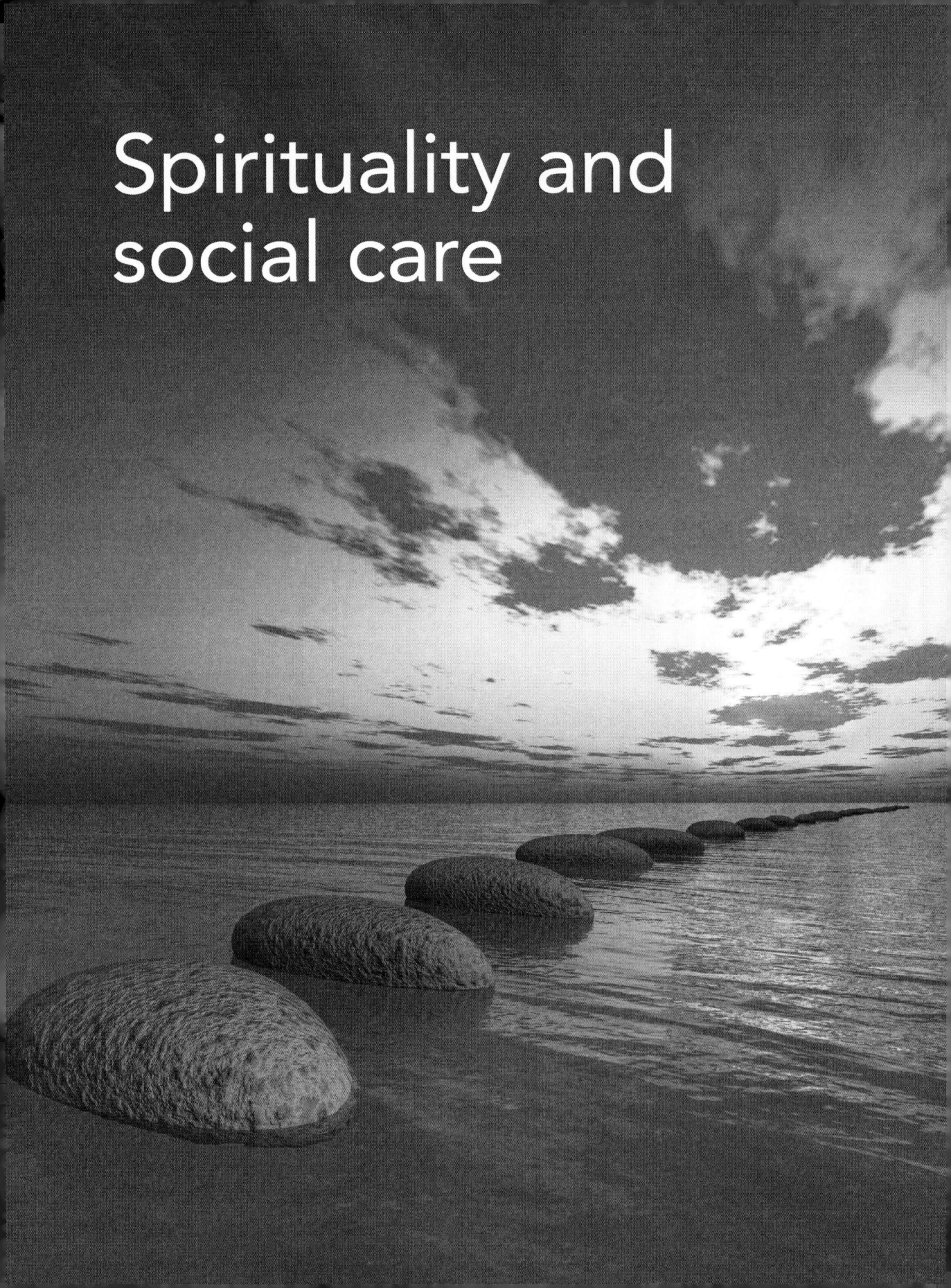

Chapter 6: Living and breathing spirituality in social work and social care

Margaret Holloway

The first time I heard Peter Gilbert speak was when he gave a keynote presentation at the Making Sense of Spirituality conference in 2007, hosted by the University of Hull's Centre for Spirituality Studies in the beautiful setting of Ravenscar on the North Yorkshire coast. He chose the title 'Breathing out – breathing in'. It quickly became clear that breathing – as both physical act and metaphorical motif – represented the essence of how Peter made sense of his personal identity and history as well as his work. Following his stepping away from senior management in the world of social care, that work was integrally bound up with pursuing the objective of making health and social care services spiritually aware, sensitive and responsive to the holistic needs of service users. For those familiar with the day-to-day business of social care services, steady rhythmic breathing is not the first image that comes to mind! As I reflect therefore on this notion which Peter bequeathed, I find myself wondering what social work and social care could look and feel like if a significant proportion of the workforce lived and breathed their spirituality.

Spirit as breath

Writers on contemporary spirituality commonly refer to its etymological origins in the Latin word *spiritus*, the Hebrew word *ru'ach* and the Greek word *pneuma* – all meaning 'breath' or 'wind' and often translated interchangeably in the Judeo-Christian tradition; for example, the book of Job refers to the 'spirit' or 'breath' of God and the book of Acts to 'wind' and 'spirit' in the story of Pentecost. The Arabic word *ruhani* also means 'spiritual'. The Zen Buddhist practice of mindfulness meditation is built on the practice of paying careful attention to each breath and, similarly, the reciting of the Qur'an is practised as both spiritual and physical exercise. This linking of spirit with breath and, by implication, of spirituality with breathing, has an important implication which is often overlooked. This is that our spirituality is an *essentially embodied experience*. Later emphases derived from Plato on the distinction between the soul and the body, which has come to be understood as the soul being the essence of the person which survives death, downplay the rich implications of living and breathing our spirituality as creatures in which body, mind and spirit are inextricably interwoven. As a runner, who knew the simultaneous importance of rhythmic breathing to his physical and spiritual fitness as well as, at times, to the ability to carry on, this was an understanding of spirituality which Peter treasured and sought always to convey.

Interestingly, however, Peter's title leads us to think of breathing out before we breathe in. A physician might describe the respiratory process as comprising first inhalation then exhalation and facilitating the exchange of gases and transfer of oxygen around the body between these two processes. Most relaxation and meditation processes, however, begin with exhalation followed by a deep breath in, and sports such as swimming place greater emphasis on getting exhalation right rather than on inhalation. We describe this slow breath out as 'emptying the lungs'. The notion of emptying oneself in order to be refilled and spiritually recharged is embedded in religious traditions and a common way to approach the discipline of 'retreat' – another foundation in Peter's own spiritual experience, as both participant and leader.

Yet how often do we apply this insight and practice to our everyday work experiences, as both individuals and organisations? In repeated inquiry reports commenting on the practice of social workers and other health professionals in the events leading up to the death of a child, rarely is the implication drawn that one of the key findings is that the professionals never found the 'space' to stand back from the relentless onslaught of frontline practice enough to draw on their own bank of personal and professional resources to assist in making the right judgement call. We speak of not having 'time to breathe' without paying attention to the clogging, clouding and sometimes toxic 'stuff' of our day-to-day business, of which we need to let go before we can function as whole, centred professionals, still less human beings. Acknowledgement may be given to training deficits, but unless the exhale–inhale rhythm of expelling, taking in, filtering, replenishing and renewing is understood, any such training will be just another set of good practice guidelines to be relegated to the 'ideal but not realistic', when the going gets tough.

Breathing in is also important, therefore. Peter often spoke of sources of *inspiration* in this respect. For him, and for many of us who debate this notion of spirituality, our inspiration is to be found in the beauty of nature, in the creative arts, in great thinkers and leaders. This may be all well and good for those of us with the education, cultural, economic and social resources to access such sources of inspiration. Finding and connecting with our personal sources of inspiration is essential for health and social care practitioners if they are to avoid burn-out (Moss, 2009). But what of those whose lives are dictated, rather, by traumatic events, unremitting social and economic stress, and who frequently suffer a range of health problems (physical and mental) which reduce still further their life opportunities? In other words, what are the sources of inspiration available to most users of social care services?

There are two important aspects to consider in responding to this question. The first is to consider what we mean by 'inspirational' and how this translates across social and cultural divides. Repeatedly in my own research I have come back to the meanings which infuse everyday life and which enable individuals (and communities, though these have not been the subject of my research) to transcend their suffering. By transcend I do not mean, 'make the best of', since there are situations and circumstances which should never be passively accepted and which social work has a duty to challenge on behalf of those we seek to help and, importantly, work to support them in achieving change in their own lives. Such 'empowerment' is a fundamental dimension of spiritual practice in the caring professions. The most skilled practitioner cannot, however, change the bald facts of a childhood robbed of its innocent trust by an abusive parent, of the vicious attack which leaves enduring physical, psychological and emotional scars, of the cruel illness which appears to take away all that is necessary to enjoy living. Yet remarkable stories of human courage and healing in the face of adversity bear testament to the fact that it is possible to transcend such experiences. In our world, Nelson Mandela has provided the most powerful example of transcendence and his legacy is to continue to inspire millions. What I mean therefore by 'transcendence' is that the oppressive and damaging circumstance or event ceases to hold that power over the essential person (Holloway & Moss, 2010). Central to this transformation taking place is that the person is able to find and draw on sources of meaning in their life.

In a study of spirituality in contemporary funerals, we found that there were three parts to this process of meaning-making: meaning-seeking, meaning-creating and meaning-taking (Holloway *et al*, 2013). It is in journeying with the person through that process that the practitioner is privileged to assist with 'breathing in' and it leads us to the final part of the trilogy which Peter used in his 'breathing out – breathing in' framework: that spiritual, or 'whole person' practice should also be *aspirational* (Gilbert, 2011). This meaning-making process can be mapped across the three elements identified (Holloway, 2012) as comprising the common ground of humanistic spirituality (see also Nolan & Holloway, 2013, for a discussion of humanistic spirituality): that it is concerned with meaning; that it is experienced in relationship and relatedness; and that it promotes certain behaviours and practices, including towards the other person. Contrast this with the uncomfortable fact that social workers frequently struggle to engage with service users who find their lives meaningless, who feel alienated from their families and the professionals they encounter, often on an involuntary basis, and whose behaviour is frequently destructive towards themselves and others. Yet the core values and principles which underpin social work intervention match closely those core elements of humanistic spirituality: in its partnership approach, social work seeks to establish what the service user defines as important and having value; emphasis is placed on establishing and working through a relationship with the service user; and social work adheres to a clear code of conduct which frames both rights and responsibilities (Holloway, 2012).

Grainger (1998) suggests that: *'Religion answers a need for meaning, order, purpose; but it is not itself that need ... it is one expression of a kind of thinking which is in fact characteristic of human mental processes, but which we become more than usually aware of in situations of existential challenge.'* (p95)

This argument is even more apt when applied to the broader terrain of spirituality. It was very apparent in the funerals study that facing the death of someone close – or in some instances, not so close – instigated an intense period of establishing, representing and experiencing the meaning of (this) life in death. This was irrespective of the age of the person or type of death, and it was happening within individuals, through their coming together in relationship as a community of mourners and through their strong need to 'do the right thing' by the person who had died. People did not speak so much of their spirituality as enact it. Likewise in the routine of social work practice, it often takes a crisis, sometimes 'hitting rock-bottom', for the service user to be open to change and if this change is to be growth-promoting the worker's role may be to help people identify those existing or potential sources of meaning and strength in their lives. This is no less the case when the crisis is not so much a response to an acute event as the exhaustion and dispiriting experience of simply carrying on or coping with setbacks. A strengths perspective (Pacquette, 2006; Saleebey, 2005) seeks to foster resilience (Ungar, 2008; Williams, 2007) including what I have referred to elsewhere as *'maintaining the spirit'* (Lloyd [Holloway], 2002). These approaches, common to social work although practitioners are not always conscious of what they are doing or of its significance, play a vital part in 'breathing in' – both for the service user and for the worker.

The 'place' in me

From the branch of eco-spiritualities we can gain further understanding of what it means to live and breathe a spirituality which is both embodied and transcendent. Aboriginal writings convey a sense of oneness with place which nurtures, sustains and heals:

'…a people rooted in the land over time have exchanged their tears, their breath, their bones, all of their elements … with their habitat many times over' (Spretnak, 1991, quoted in Zapf, 2005, p637).

Discovery of the sacred in the natural environment is part and parcel of contemporary spiritualities and New Age religions in the West, but we are some way from fully nurturing this sense of interconnectedness between self and communities and their built environments, including those in which we seek to care for vulnerable and sick individuals and rehabilitate them back into their own environment, or those who have transgressed societal laws and moral codes. Attention to the caring environment has been given some prominence in recent years (Waller & Finn, 2011), though with rather more focus on those physical elements which are easier to 'fix' than the spiritual embeddedness suggested by the notion of 'the place in me'. Zapf (2005) expresses it thus:

'Can we come to understand our environment in spiritual terms, to appreciate and express and celebrate our connectedness? A simple yet profound question … could serve as the starting point for rethinking social work's commitment to person in environment: what does it mean to live well in this place?' (p639)

This way of understanding connectedness and relatedness, in which the natural, built and human relationship environments are experienced as a seamless whole and the sacred and holy infuses everyday life (Nolan & Holloway, 2013), represents a profound challenge to social care practice. In its complete expression it remains an aspiration, but one which could transform the way in which care transitions are managed in both emergency and routine interventions designed to promote best practice. One of Peter's oft-used notions was that of the 'travelling spiritual identity', which retains a core but develops and adapts to changing circumstances as well as to an altered sense of self. We do well to consider how to nurture that spiritual core and foster new spiritual connections as we support people along their care pathway. The realisation that most people want to die at home or in a 'homely' environment has come only out of the profound sense of alienation experienced by dying people and their families when the technological and institutional environment of the modern hospital became the default place to die. Likewise, the concept of 'ageing in place' has only just begun to be understood and facilitated (O'Connor & Pearson, 2004–5; Chiu, 2008). Caring for people in such a way that they can 'live well in this place' is as important a part of good practice as following correct procedures and it implies that we facilitate that sense of connectedness which we now recognise as a core component of spirituality.

Nurturing connections with place is as important for workers as for service users. Work environments in which humanity is embodied – in the physical surroundings, mission statements, work ethic, professional values – are places in which workers can feel whole and connections are made between the *'middles of people'* (Jordan, 1979) – as colleagues, managers and with service users. Too often the picture is entirely opposite, the environment leading to practices which are dysfunctional and alienating. One of the most powerful illustrations of this disconnectedness and alienation occurred for me in my practice as a maternity hospital social worker. In the early days of the still-birth procedure being introduced, I was summoned to the maternity ward by an agitated ward sister. With the words, 'She can't have that', she handed me the photograph of a still-born baby whose body had begun to deteriorate in the womb, the face showing signs of maceration, requesting that I talk the mother out of wanting to have the photograph. I agreed with the nurse that this was a shocking photograph, but what I saw was an unwrapped baby lying next to an overflowing rubbish bin. Clearly, whoever had taken the photo had been so out of touch with the caring task, distressed for the parents and themselves and no doubt harassed by a busy night on the delivery suite in which no one had had time to attend to clearing the rubbish, that they had failed to remember the purpose of the photograph. As I talked to the mother about the glimpse she had had of her baby, it became apparent that what she saw and grieved for, was not what the medical professionals saw. I was honest with her that the photograph we had was not the one she deserved to have as a treasured memory, and after some reflection she decided not to see it but instead I accompanied her to the mortuary where she spent time with her baby in peaceful and respectful surroundings.

Wounded healers

It is important to acknowledge here that life takes its toll on the social care worker. In the first instance, it is those very qualities of sensitivity to another's pain and distress and the capacity to acknowledge our own pain, which lead us into the profession and which enable us to reach out to service users in their daily struggles. Maintaining empathy while retaining the necessary objectivity to accurately assess complex situations, negotiate between conflicting agendas and protect vulnerable parties, not only requires a high level of skill, but is emotionally demanding. Central to Peter's spirituality and his pursuit of spiritual practice in social care, was his acknowledgement and acceptance of his own wounds. Not everyone is so open, yet we do both ourselves and those we seek to support, a disservice by failing to understand that healing and hurting are reciprocally related (Lloyd [Holloway], 1995).

The origins of the model of the 'wounded healer' can be seen in ancient Greek mythology (Nolan & Holloway, 2013) and a number of writers have applied it to modern health and social care practice (Jung, 1993; Nouwen, 1994; Kearney, 1996; Wright, 2004). Referring to work with people who are dying or bereaved, Holloway (2007) summarises: *'Very simply, it is out of shared weakness and vulnerability that the healer reaches out to heal. The model teaches us to value rather than avoid our own pain, perhaps from a similar personal experience, as the key element which enables the healer to connect and communicate with the dying or bereaved person'* (p178)

In contrast to its growing use in palliative care, the notion of the wounded healer is not widely applied in frontline social work practice, despite the prevalence of partnership models and an increasing trend for former service users to train as social workers. There seems to be a residual fear of 'over-identification' with the service user and the equation of 'good practice' with confident decision-making on the part of strong professionals. This is to misunderstand the nature and sources of our strength. A number of religious spiritual traditions (in contrast, it must be said, to much of the popular contemporary self-actualising discourse) subscribe to the rather different view contained within St. Paul's words, *'When I am weak, then am I strong'* (2 Corinthians 12:10). As social work in the UK progresses through the latest overhaul of training set off by the scrutiny and soul-searching which arose after the case of 'Baby Peter', this element is in danger of being missed. That is, that practice competence develops as much from understanding and drawing on our own vulnerability and sources of strength as it does from specific skills training. Social care is a human services workforce and we can ill afford to neglect the dimension of being human. This belongs to the terrain of nurturing our shared spirituality, as individuals and within teams.

Conclusion

Social work and social care is tasked with intervening in people's lives to support them in difficult circumstances, to help bring about change and to address particular problems and problematic behaviours. Canda and Furman remind us that spiritually sensitive practice *'...includes but is more than problem solving. It includes but is more than promoting coping, adapting, or recovery ... spiritually sensitive practice identifies people's talents, skills, capacities, and resources and mobilises them in the service of both their immediate goals and their highest aspirations and potentials'* (Canda & Furman, 2010, p315).

In the UK, we are currently charged with implementing the 'Transforming Services' agenda, intended to return us to the service user, in control of their own lives, as the starting point for designing and delivering services (DH, 2006). Yet for change to be truly transformational, it must do more than turn around the model of service delivery. It must courageously engage with the human condition. Connecting with our own spirituality and the spirituality of the other person offers us a foundation from which to venture into such a challenging terrain. It reminds us that spiritual care and social justice and responsibility are inextricably linked; that empowerment implies transcending and thereby transforming the conditions of our everyday lives; that spiritual liberation is the key to overcoming addictive, compulsive and harmful patterns of behaviour. Living and breathing spirituality in social work and social care would, as Sheridan (2004) so powerfully expressed it, *'nurture the soul of social work'*. As I reflect on the struggles of social work in the UK, about which Peter cared so deeply, I conclude that the profession must reconnect with its soul if it is to rise to current challenges.

References

Canda E & Furman L (2010) *Spiritual Diversity in Social Work Practice: The heart of helping (2nd edition)*. New York: The Free Press.

Chui E (2008) Introduction to Special Issue on Ageing in Place. *Ageing International* **32** 165–166.

Department of Health (2006) *Our Health, Our Care, Our Say: A new direction for community services*. London: Crown Copyright.

Gilbert P (2011) Understanding mental health and spirituality. In P Gilbert (ed) *Spirituality and Mental Health*. Brighton: Pavilion Publishing.

Grainger R (1998) *The Social Symbolism of Grief and Mourning*. London: Jessica Kingsley.

Holloway M (2007) *Negotiating Death in Contemporary Health and Social Care*. Bristol: Policy Press.

Holloway M (2012) Social work. In M Cobb, C Puchalski & B Rumbold (eds) *Oxford Textbook of Spirituality in Healthcare* (pp235–241). Oxford: Oxford University Press.

Holloway M & Moss B (2010) *Spirituality and Social Work*. Basingstoke: Palgrave Macmillan.

Holloway M, Adamson S, Argyrou V, Draper P & Mariau D (2013) "Funerals aren't nice but it couldn't have been nicer": the makings of a good funeral. *Mortality* **18** (1) 30–53.

Jordan B (1979) *Helping in Social work*. London: Routledge & Kegan Paul Books.

Jung CG (1993) *The Practice of Psychotherapy* (Collected Works of CG Jung Volume 16) (2nd edition). London: Routledge.

Kearney M (1996) *Mortally Wounded: Stories of soul pain, death and healing*. Dublin: Marino Books.

Lloyd M [M Holloway] (1995) *Embracing the Paradox: Pastoral care with dying and bereaved people*. Contact Pastoral Monographs No 5. Edinburgh: Contact Pastoral Limited Trust.

Lloyd M [M Holloway] (2002) A framework for working with loss. In N. Thompson (ed.) *Loss and Grief: A Guide for Human Services Practitioners*, pp208–220. London: Palgrave.

Moss B (2009) Spirituality in the workplace. In N Thompson and J Bates (eds) *Workplace Well-Being: A critical approach*. Basingstoke: Palgrave.

Nolan S & Holloway M (2013) *A–Z of Spirituality*. Basingstoke: Palgrave.

Nouwen H (1994) *The Wounded Healer: Ministry in contemporary society* (2nd edition). London: Darton, Longman & Todd.

O'Connor M & Pearson A (2004-5) Ageing in place – dying in place: competing discourses for care of the dying in aged care policy. *Australian Journal of Advanced Nursing* **22** (2) 32–38.

Pacquette M (2006) The science of happiness. *Perspectives in Psychiatric Care* **42** (1) 1–2.

Saleebey D (ed) (2005) *The Strengths Perspective in Social Work Practice* (4th edition) Boston: Pearson/ Allyn & Bacon.

Sheridan M (2004) If we nurtured the soul of social work. *Society for Spirituality and Social Work* **4** (2) 3.

Ungar M (2008) Resilience across Cultures. *British Journal of Social Work* **38** (2) 218–235.

Waller S & Finn H (2011) Improving the Patient Experience – Environments for care at end of life. The King's Fund's Enhancing the Healing Environment Programme 2008–2010. Available at: www.kingsfund.org.uk/publications/environments-care-end-life (accessed January 2014).

Williams C (2007) On a path of most resilience. *Community Care* **16** (1686) 20–1.

Wright M (2004) Hospice care and models of spirituality. *European Journal of Palliative Care* **11** (2) 75–78.

Zapf MK (2005) The spiritual dimension of person and environment: perspectives from social work and traditional knowledge. *International Social Work* **48** (5) 633–642.

Chapter 7: It's humanity, stoopid! Humanity, spirituality and social work education

Bernard Moss

Setting the scene

With characteristic humour and penetrating insight Peter Gilbert chose the title 'It's humanity, stoopid!' for his inaugural professorial lecture in 2005 to celebrate his appointment as professor of social work at Staffordshire University. This arresting populist phrase captured for him something of the troubling context in which the social work profession had found itself. Time and again examples had occurred of children and vulnerable adults being subjected to serious abuse; time and again social workers had found themselves in the media spotlight and the public gaze for sins both of omission and commission, and morale was in sharp decline. For Peter, there was a common theme that ran through all of this, a theme that united those who used services and those who provided them; those who cared and those who were cared for; colleagues in very senior management positions (Peter knew from his own experience what that entailed), and those who were marginalised, oppressed and stigmatised in our society (Peter's own experience of depression enriched his insight into these issues). That theme was our common shared humanity, a theme that encapsulates the core values of social work, and provides a litmus test for how we treat each other, no matter what roles we fulfil.

The irony and indeed the tragedy of all of this is that Peter felt the need to re-state what was so obvious, so central, and so fundamental to any aspect of people work. Of course, it is all about people working with people, dealing with people, respecting each other as people, even when difficult and challenging decisions have to be taken to protect vulnerable children and adults! And yet this is so often not how it felt, and his call for a deeper awareness of our innate spirituality

– what makes us tick, to use his lovely phrase – is a profound reminder that we ignore our essential humanity at our peril, most especially if we belong to a profession such as social work.

Several years later, much has changed and nothing has changed.

The feeling that nothing has changed is fuelled by further tragedies not just in social work but in the wider field of health and social care. At the time of writing (mid 2013) the tragic (sadly, this powerful word is having to be used so often that there is a risk of its impact being devalued: 'here we go again, another tragic case that should never have happened') story of the murder of Daniel Pelka by his mother and stepfather has seared the media front pages. Once again, we are aghast at the enormity of the abuse, and how and why it was not prevented when (apart from others who might have been informally involved) many professionals appeared not to have noticed that something so serious was wrong.

And there is more. The NHS is reeling not just from the Stafford Hospital debacle, but from further reports elsewhere in the country where patients' lives are being put seriously at risk. In his letter to the Secretary of State introducing his review into the quality of care and treatment in our NHS hospitals, professor Sir Bruce Keogh made the powerful and telling observation that: *'the NHS embodies the social conscience of our country'* (Keogh, 2013).

In his own way, Keogh was echoing what Peter had been saying about social work: that there is a core issue here about our values and the extent to which we respect and value our common humanity especially at times when we are vulnerable, sick and at risk. To have to remind ourselves that care and compassion are the *sine qua non* of any and every aspect of people work should be massively unnecessary: the fact that it has become an urgent necessity is an appalling indictment of many of the services being offered.

Keogh goes on to comment upon how he found: *'limited understanding of how important and how simple it can be to genuinely listen to the views of patients and staff, and to engage them in how to improve services.'* (2013)

It seems at times as if, in spite of all the decades of imploring that we should never allow such tragedies to happen again, the one thing we can be certain of is that they will assuredly happen again.

And yet, out of some of these tragic stories, good things have begun to emerge. The Government and professional reactions to the death Peter Connelly (Baby P) have led to the formation of The College of Social Work (TCSW) with a remit for professional excellence and the driving up of standards. Jo Cleary, chair of TCSW, noted that: *'There have always been many excellent conscientious social workers, but we are now moving towards a situation where every social worker without exception falls into this category.'* (TCSW website, 2013)

There is an increased emphasis upon developing sound, mature, professional judgement within the social work profession following the seminal report by Eileen Munro (2011). Furthermore, the new Professional Capabilities Framework for all social workers (irrespective of their place within the hierarchy), requiring evidence of the impact of their continuing professional development upon their professional practice during each and every two-year period before re-registration, is evidence of the profession taking seriously the challenges it currently faces.

All these developments are important because, as Peter said, *It's humanity, stoopid!* – if we don't get these basics right, then the rest won't fall into place, or more worryingly, will be built upon insecure foundations. There are, nevertheless, some important challenges to be faced, not least in the way that social workers are trained, and the extent to which social work education is laying the best foundations for excellent future practice. It is to a discussion of these issues that we now turn.

Challenges for social work education and training

The range of social work education and training provision has seen a rapid expansion in recent years. The traditional full-time three-year undergraduate/ two-year postgraduate range of programmes, together with part-time opportunities, delivered by higher education institutions has been expanded by various employment-based routes, at the forefront of which has been the Open University. More recently, in the wake of the Baby P scandal, and the demand for higher-qualified social work professionals, the Government has introduced a 'fast track' qualification in children and families social work called Step Up to Social Work. This programme is available to candidates with first class or upper second class degrees. Originally offering a master's degree in 18 months, it was later modified to a postgraduate certificate achievable in 14 months. Another initiative called Frontline aims to produce qualified workers in 12 months.

There are several questions that arise from these developments. How long does it/should it take to educate and train someone in readiness to become a newly qualified social worker? What is the difference between training and education in this context? What would be missing if the education aspect were to be withdrawn?

Is there room for the current diversity of programmes, or is Governmental pressure going to increase the number of shorter-length programmes?

Even more fundamental, however, is the question of how social work values are taught and absorbed so that they underpin the whole social work enterprise. Are the core values which include 'respecting our shared humanity' taught in such a way that they will always inform and underpin excellent practice? This crucial issue, which is at the very heart of social work, and is also seen so clearly in all of Peter's contributions to our understanding and practice, deserves further discussion. The rest of this chapter, therefore, will explore briefly four 'strands' to this discussion to show how each strand opens up important opportunities to embed the value base of respecting our shared humanity in our education, training and practice. These four strands are:

1. Engaging with the Professional Capabilities Framework

2. A commitment to social justice

3. The role of humour

4. Understanding spirituality.

Engaging with the Professional Capabilities Framework (PCF)

With the arrival of The College of Social Work (TCSW) the scenery around social work's education, training and continuing professional development has been significantly re-shaped, as part of the drive towards raising standards and achieving excellence. A new framework has been established which enables everyone involved in the profession to locate themselves and identify how they need to progress, from the day they are selected for training, to their first day as a newly qualified social worker, and then throughout the rest of their careers, no matter what role or position they achieve. The framework reflects the increasing complexity of the social work role, and the developing capabilities, knowledge and skills that are necessary to meet the professional and personal demands of the work. As Figure 7.1 illustrates, there are nine domains involved, with dividing lines between the various domains being purely illustrative, as every domain ultimately overlaps and interacts with the others within the rich complexity of practice.

The imagery of the 'fan', which becomes broader the further one progresses into a social work career, is a powerful pictorial reminder that each domain is relevant throughout a social worker's career. Indeed, each of them has a particular relevance at every stage, including middle and senior management and all leadership roles. At each and every point in a career trajectory the PCF outlines some of the key 'markers' that need to be achieved, and indicates where evidence needs to be provided every two years for each of the nine domains, in order to be re-registered by the Health and Care Professions Council (HCPC), the regulatory body for social work.

Figure 7.1: Professional Capabilities Framework for social workers

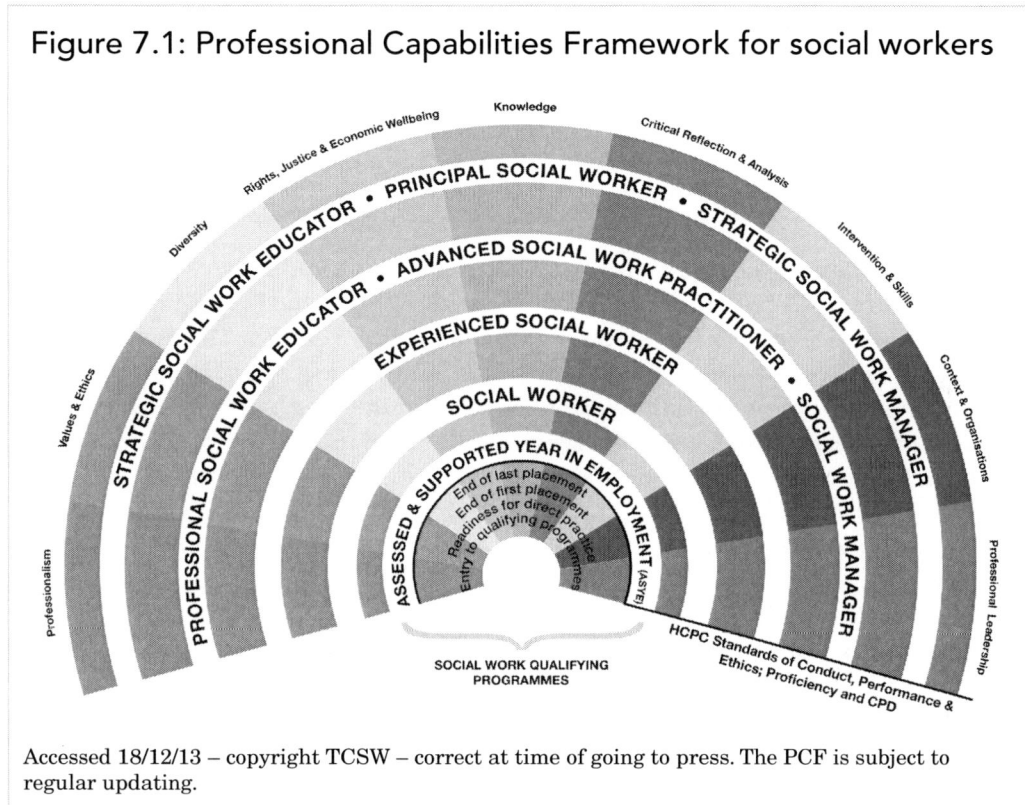

Accessed 18/12/13 – copyright TCSW – correct at time of going to press. The PCF is subject to regular updating.

For a detailed study of the PCF, an interactive version is available on the TCSW website where all the additional information relevant to each domain can be easily accessed.

For the purposes of this discussion, two points deserve particular mention. First, there is a specific domain dedicated to values and ethics throughout a social work career. This provides an ongoing opportunity for everyone to reflect carefully on the ways in which social work values are put into practice every day, and what particular challenges this commitment raises. Second, as is to be expected, the value base of respecting our common humanity runs through, and has relevance to, each and every domain on the PCF. Excellent social work practice cannot be achieved without this commitment.

This framework provides a thought-provoking opportunity for social work education to lay important foundations for future practice, knowing that this will be in place throughout the students' future careers as a benchmark for their continuing excellence, and a relentless commitment to core social work values in which everyone's core humanity is respected.

A commitment to social justice

Social workers are very familiar with what has for many years been called the 'care and control' dimension to practice. But this is far from the whole story, as TCSW's commitment to social justice makes clear. Holloway and Moss (2010, p149–150) point out that:

'[This commitment is also] enshrined in various professional statements. Hodge (2007) refers to the National Association of Social Workers in the USA and notes that, 'Social justice is a central social work value' (NASW, 1999). The British Association of Social Workers' Code of Ethics (2002), having re-affirmed the fundamental value, dignity and worth of every human being, goes on to stress the importance of social justice, emphasising, 'the fair and equitable distribution of resources to meet basic human needs', together with, the pursuit of social justice [that] involves identifying, seeking to alleviate and advocating strategies for overcoming structural disadvantage (3.2.1).'

Furthermore, the definition of social work adopted by the International Federation of Social Workers, and the International Association of Schools of Social Work includes the following statement:

'The social work profession promotes social change, problem-solving in human relationships and the empowerment and liberation of people to enhance well-being… principles of human rights and social justice are fundamental to social work.' (2004)

The implications of these core values are considerable, and represent an ongoing challenge to all social work educators and practitioners. But for the purpose of this chapter they make abundantly clear the shared, corporate community-based nature of social work. In terms of what makes us 'tick' (to use Peter's phrase); what gives us our meaning and purpose, and what drives us each day to help improve the 'lot' of those with whom we are privileged to work – these values represent the heart, soul and spirit of who we are.

It remains one of the core challenges of social work education to explore the challenges of social justice. To its credit, the PCF discussed earlier provides an excellent starting point for this exploration of an important strand in our common shared humanity.

The role of humour

There is a useful 'rule of thumb' about the use of humour in social work practice: if in doubt, don't! There is nothing worse than a joke misfiring, or a comment intended to be light-hearted being taken the wrong way and causing hurt and dismay. On the other hand, if used wisely, it can be a very humanising, levelling moment, where two (or more) human beings share laughter together. It takes them to a different level in their relationship, and can break down some of the barriers that prevent important work being undertaken.

In the education and training context it is perhaps somewhat easier to take the risks. Peter was always willing to do that in his teaching. His ability to find the right cartoon to illustrate a point was renowned. Amongst his favourites was the cartoon depicting a somewhat down-and-out man slouching on the sofa while his wife read out a letter to him which said, 'It's from the University of Life – you didn't get in!' Another favourite was of the Sistine Chapel where an embittered cleaning lady was berating Michaelangelo: 'Never mind your ceiling; look at the mess you've made of my floor!' With these, and other telling cartoons taken from *Private Eye* or the famous *Clare in the Community* series, Peter was able to engage students at depth and to explore underlying values and assumptions that permeate social work practice.

Difficult and painful topics often attract a humorous response from comedians, not as a way of trivialising issues but on the contrary providing a way into topics that seem at first to be impenetrable. To edge into the impenetrable is an important skill for social work practice, and we need to be comfortable with exploring difficult and challenging emotional issues ourselves so that we can engage at this level with others. Used judiciously and sensitively, humour can sometimes offer a way in, so long as the result is a recognition and celebration of our common shared humanity and not a 'putting down' of the person in pain.

Understanding spirituality

Peter's great contribution to our understanding of spirituality and its relevance to social work (and all people work) deserves deep celebration. Through his teaching, research and wide-ranging publications particularly in relation to mental health and well-being, his insights and commitment to this great theme shines through.

His argument (shared within a burgeoning literature on this theme) is that our spirituality, whether it has a secular or religious dimension to it, encapsulates who we are and what gives us a sense of meaning, purpose, value and vision for our living and our loving. It is not a neat compartmentalised topic of interest to quicken the pulse of a tiny minority, but of little relevance to everyone else. It is rather the litmus test of our humanity, and shows us in our true colours.

In his well-respected edited volume *Spirituality and Mental Health* (2011), Peter states this clearly:

'Spirituality, in whatever form it takes, is a vital dimension of our humanity. As disillusionment with robotic and mechanistic forms of care has set it, and our society has become more multifaceted and multicultural, spirituality is becoming of increasing importance in health and social care.' (p42)

Spirituality therefore can rightly be regarded as being fundamentally important to our common shared humanity.

Conclusion

This chapter has explored some of core themes for social work education and training arising out of the value base of respecting our common shared humanity. It has been argued that, sadly, a re-affirmation of this core value base of people work has become increasingly necessary in recent years, and that without it people will not receive the quality of care to which they are entitled. The Professional Capabilities Framework for social work has the potential to insist on the supremacy of the values that are needed to underpin excellent practice, including the wider dimensions of social justice. The human side of education and training in people work can often emerge through a gentle use of humour to take us to a deeper level, and the importance of an understanding of spirituality underpins our common shared humanity. Peter, as always, put it in a nutshell: *It's humanity, stoopid!*

References

British Association of Social Workers (2002) *The Code of Ethics for Social Work*. Birmingham: BASW.

Gilbert P (2011) *Spirituality and Mental Health: A handbook for service users, carers and staff wishing to bring a spiritual dimension to mental health services*. Brighton: Pavilion.

Hodge DR (2007) Social justice and people of faith: a transnational perspective. *National Association of Social Workers–Social Work* **52** (2).

Holloway M & Moss B (2010) *Spirituality and Social Work*. Basingstoke: Palgrave Macmillan.

International Association of Schools of Social Work (IASSW) and the International Federation of Social Work (IFSW) (2004) *International Declaration of Ethical Principles of Social Work and International Ethical Standards for Social Work*. Bern, Switzerland: IASSW/IFSWO.

Keogh B (2013) *Review into the quality of care and treatment provided by 14 Hospital Trusts in England: Overview Report*. London: NHS England.

Munro E (2011) *The Munro Review of Child Protection: Final Report. A child centred system*. London: Department of Education.

National Association of Social Workers (1999) *The NASW Code of Ethics*. Washington, DC: NASW.

The College of Social Work (2013) The serious case review into the Daniel Pelka case will have lessons for all professionals [online] Available at: http://www.tcsw.org.uk/standard-2col-rhm-blog.aspx?id=8589935052 (accessed December 2013).

Further reading

Gilbert P (2010) *Social Work and Mental Health: The value of everything*. Lyme Regis: Russell House Publishing.

Gilbert P (2013) *Spirituality and End of Life Care: A handbook for service users, carers and staff wishing to bring a spiritual dimension to palliative care*. Hove: Pavilion.

Holloway M & Moss B (2010) *Spirituality and Social Work*. Basingstoke: Palgrave Macmillan.

International Federation of Social Workers (2001) *The Definition of Social Work*. Berne: IFSW.

IASSW International Association of Schools of Social Work (IASSW) and the International Federation of Social Work (IFSW) (2004) *International Declaration of Ethical Principles of Social Work and International Ethical Standards for Social Work*. Bern, Switzerland: IASSW/IFSW.

Moss B (2013) The caring professions: The social worker. Chapter 15. In: P Gilbert (Ed) *Spirituality and End of Life Care*. Hove: Pavilion.

Chapter 8: Spirituality, listening to the service user's story, compassion and an ethic of care

Margaret McGettrick

The Dalai Lama's definition of compassion is: *'sensitivity to the suffering of self and others with a deep commitment to try to relieve it'* (in Gilbert, 2011b).

Recently, 'compassion' has been missing from our healthcare services. This has been highlighted by the scandals at Winterbourne View and Mid Staffordshire Hospital. The Government has responded speedily and has made a commitment in its report *Compassion in Practice* (2012), to focus on delivering *'high quality compassionate care'* as well as *'quality of treatment'* from within a compassionate and caring culture. The Government proposes to promote six 'Cs. These are *'care, compassion, competence, communication, courage and commitment'* (DH, 2012).

An 'ethic' has been described as *'a way of living which seeks to train people in its art'* (Hayes, 2013). 'Care' has been described as *'altruistic love … that seeks to benefit the valued other for his or her own sake … bringing about his or her welfare'* (Callahan, 2001). In *Compassion in Practice* (DH, 2012), the Government proposes what might be called 'an ethic of care', which is a suggested programme of activities that will encourage care givers to learn about and practice compassionate care.

In his personal and professional life, Peter Gilbert demonstrated a genuine sensitivity to the suffering of others. He was and remained a service user himself. In his last address to the National Spirituality and Mental Health Forum (NSMHF), he spoke of the importance of giving people permission to tell their stories. He told us of Davina, whom he met during a presentation to the Sikh community in Birmingham. Peter listened to Davina's story and was moved to tears by it. Davina was touched by Peter's tears. She said that nobody had ever cried with her before. Peter later went on to talk about compassion and the profound need that we all have for a sense of value, of being respected, of being responded to and of having the feeling that 'we matter'.

This chapter brings together and explores three themes that were of particular interest to Peter and which are of relevance to this new government initiative. These themes are spirituality, listening to the service user's story and compassion.

Spirituality

The first theme is spirituality. Peter travelled widely throughout the country on behalf of the NSMHF, explaining and exploring the importance of spirituality in mental health.

The term 'spirituality' is a relatively new term. It is concerned *'with finding a deep-seated source of meaning and purpose in life, especially during hardship, through a journey that continues in stages of increasing maturity throughout life'* (Culliford, 2011). For some people, this may involve a search for the sacred or for the transcendent.

Research suggests that one's spirituality (defined as faith) is a developmental process which progresses over time from selfish immaturity to an altruistic, compassionate mature stage, which is characterised by selfless and inclusive service. It is estimated that eight per cent of the population have reached a mature stage of development capable of such compassionate caring.

The contemporary NHS is going through a period of change. It has moved from a purely medical model, through person-centred care to the current recovery model. In the medical model, the focus of care was mainly on cure, while care was considered to be something that happened when 'cure' was not possible. Person-centred care recognises that service users have needs other than physical ones. Some of these needs have been identified as the loss of self-esteem, identity, meaning, purpose and also isolation. Peter spoke of how, when depressed, he felt disconnected from himself, other people and God.

The recovery model, which is now government policy, emerged in the 1990s and was influenced by the success of survivor self-help groups, whose members demonstrated that it was possible to live well with their symptoms, when cure was not possible. 'Recovery' doesn't have a universally accepted definition. An attractive one however, is *'to live well with your symptoms'* (Brown & Kindirikirira, 2008).

A key feature of recovery is the recovery of meaning and purpose. Spirituality and recovery are interconnected, since they are both concerned with the search for meaning.

Attention to spirituality is important to service users in recovery and efforts are being made to introduce spiritual care assessments into the care planning process.

Listening to the service user's story

The second theme of this chapter is listening to the service user's story. Peter said that one of the things that helped him the most when he was depressed was a GP *'who really listened attentively'* (Gilbert, 2011a).

There are a number of reasons why it is important to listen to a service user's story.
- It conveys dignity and respect.
- It assists with identity formation.
- It assists with the meaning-making process.
- It is a way to express needs.

Listening to the service user's story reveals to them that their story matters, that it is worth listening to and that they are valued. It therefore enhances their self-esteem. It makes them feel cared for and ends their sense of isolation. It thus supports and promotes the NHS Constitution's value of respect and dignity.

Kate, a former service user, shares something of her experience of not being listened to and how this affected her: *'I've had many years in the mental health system. It was not helpful to me. The biggest problem I found was with the professionals. They don't want to hear about people's life stories. I'm a survivor. I might not have done so much self-harming if only someone had listened to me. But they don't, which makes you feel like they don't care. Sometimes pills are not the answer. Talking is much better. It's recognition. To hear my story is to hear who I am. When you're in care and have no family you feel like a non-individual. You need someone to listen.'*

Kate's story highlights the importance of being listened to in her search for a positive sense of self.

A person's identity is formed from a combination of three factors. It is primarily formed through autobiographical storytelling in which key events over time are selected and joined together. To do this requires a storyteller and a story listener.

As Kate's story has highlighted, many of our service users have never had anyone to listen to their story, and consequently run the risk of not knowing who they are. Men and women tell their stories differently. Women tend to tell their stories in a fragmented way and use emotion. Men tell their stories in a more linear way and are more factual. This storytelling may need to be repeated many times until the identity-forming task is complete.

Identity is also, in part, a social construction, formed from the opinions expressed by key authority figures. Family members or care givers themselves may impart to service users a negative self-image through the words they use about them.

Personal choice is also a factor in identity formation. The service user is free to choose which factors they will include in the process and how they interpret them. This is important, particularly for 'recovery', because the service user can change their sense of self by looking at the past differently or by reviewing it in the light of current thinking. This knowledge has led to the recent growth of narrative therapy, which helps service users to choose a more positive sense of self.

Listening to the service user's story helps the person to find meaning in their lives. Peter said that *'human beings are meaning-making creatures'* (Gilbert, 2013). Whenever a person tells their story, they are also searching for meaning and the story will continue to be told until its meaning has been disclosed. Meaning-making requires both storytelling and a framework of reference. Such a framework was traditionally provided by a person's culture, often in the form of a religious belief system. In their religious stories, myths, symbols, worship practices and traditions, people searched for and found answers to the important questions of life such as: Who am I? Where did I come from? Where am I going? What am I doing here? Why is there suffering in the world and what happens when I die?

Bryan Stone explains (1996): *'Spirituality is the process of discovering meaning in and making meaning out of the whole of our lives … it is the ongoing journey of integrating the entire texture of our everyday and ordinary living into what we take to be the whole in which we find ourselves … Some such whole operates in all our lives, regardless of whether we understand it to include God or not. Thus there is … a Buddhist spirituality, a Hindu spirituality or even a Marxist spirituality.'*

Spirituality and religion were once considered inseparable, but in our contemporary society they have become separated. Many people have rejected religious institutions with their doctrines, dogmas and claims to universal truth. They have chosen instead to validate truth through personal experience and conscience. This has resulted in many 'postmodern' people deciding to be spiritual but not religious, or as Grace Davie (1994) coined the phrase, they *'believe without belonging'*. Many people today, therefore, have no framework for meaning-making, which has resulted in them experiencing their lives as meaningless.

Recent research by Michael King explored this phenomenon. According to a recent article by Vernon (2013), King *et al's* research recognised three categories of people:

1. those with a 'religious' understanding of life (35%)

2. those with a 'spiritual' understanding of life (19%)

3. those who have neither a 'spiritual' nor a 'religious' understanding of life (46%).

King *et al's* research showed that people with only a 'spiritual' understanding of life were particularly vulnerable to experiencing mental health problems (Vernon, 2013).

Listening to the service user's story is important because it is the way they make care givers aware of their needs.

Compassion

The third theme of this chapter is compassion. The NHS Constitution enshrined compassion as one of its six key organisational and personal values, which were to guide the NHS in the 21st century and it is one of the six C's outlined in *Compassion in Practice* (2012).

We live in a plural society and compassion is a common value shared by all the major world religions. Because of this, it has been suggested that a new spirituality is emerging, 'the spirituality of compassion'.

Compassion has been variously described as a quality of love, a value, a virtue, a lifestyle choice, a response to need, a feeling or emotion, a motivating force, a commitment to action, a fulfilling practice and for some it is also described as a spiritual practice. As a value, it is a quality considered to be good and useful.

Compassion is also a virtue which is considered to be a good and useful quality in a person. As such, it can be learnt. Practise of it can become habitual so that it becomes part of a person's personality. Such persons become 'compassionate people'.

Compassion happens as part of a three-step process of noticing, feeling and doing. The first part of the process requires the care giver to notice the service user's need. Attentive listening to the service user's story helps the care giver to both see and hear, through verbal and non-verbal cues, the needs of the service user.

This recognition of need triggers an emotional response or feeling in the observant care giver. The feeling may be one of pity, sympathy for, kindness towards, or empathy with, the person in need. Empathy is the feeling of suffering with the service user. Empathy leads to a sense of solidarity with the person being cared for. At this stage, the care giver can make a choice to act or not on their feelings.

The choice to act is associated with compassion. Compassion is not just a feeling, but it is a force or a compulsion to act. The choice the care giver makes will depend on a number of factors, which include the particularity of the circumstances, the context of the care, the health and safety of all involved, boundary issues and the care giver's stage of spiritual maturity.

The action may be simple or complex. It may be a smile, a gentle touch, a kind word or a compassionate act of service. It may require the care giver to become an advocate on behalf of the service user. It may ultimately involve taking action for social justice. In some circumstances, it may require considerable courage as, for example, when a care giver becomes a whistleblower.

For many care givers, compassion has become a lifestyle. They have, through practise, become compassionate people. They are rewarded with joy and a sense of fulfilment in their work. For many, this compassionate lifestyle is what motivated them to work in healthcare and continues to motivate their daily practice. It becomes a source of meaning and purpose for them, guiding the way they choose to live their lives.

For some care givers, compassion is a form of spiritual practice, which leads to an encounter with the sacred. For the Christian care giver, empathy and compassion are understood to be qualities of love. God is love and indwells every person's spirit. Empathy and compassion are understood therefore, as qualities of the love of God which flows through the care giver to the one being cared for. They are God's properties and express how God feels for the person in need. Compassion is God's authority for the care giver to act. The care giver acts as God's servant, fulfilling His promise to be present with all people, at all times, suffering with them.

Because of the power and presence of the Holy Spirit, this love has the power of transcendence. Every time a person knows or loves someone, they enter into their spirit, where they both know and are known by God. This brings a sense of love, joy and peace as they experience an encounter with the living God.

When a Christian reaches out in love to another in an act of service, or to communicate with them, the power of love enables them to transcend and unite with the spirit of the other. The other is touched by the love of God flowing through the care giver. It is a communion of love in which there is a reciprocal giving and receiving of the love of God to and from both. In this way the Christian care giver fulfils their commission to love God and neighbour in order to inherit eternal life.

Compassion in Practice (2012) speaks of the importance of strong leadership and of the need to give *'staff time to learn, reflect and re-energise'* (DH, 2012).

In his last address to the NSMHF, Peter said that leaders *'need to listen to people's stories; they need to demonstrate compassion and must live the values they propose'*. Peter has given us an example of such leadership. His many meetings, presentations and workshops to NHS mental health trusts throughout the country, his personal compassionate encounters, together with the many books he wrote, will continue to influence the minds and hearts of those who knew him or who have come to know him through his writings, for many years to come. Peter understood the importance of spirituality in the lives of service users. He knew first hand the importance of being listened to and he made the time to be compassionate. He valued everyone he met and made each person feel that they mattered.

The author hopes that pausing to reflect on these three themes, which Peter valued so highly, will inspire the reader to incorporate them into their own leadership and personal care practices. In this way, it is hoped that this chapter will contribute to the successful implementation of compassion in practice in the 21st century NHS.

References

Brown W & Kindirikirira N (2008) *Recovering Mental Health in Scotland*. Glasgow: Scottish Recovery Network.

Callahan S (2001) The psychology of emotion and the ethics of Care. In: Diana Fritz Cates and Paul Lauritzen (Eds) *Medicine and the Ethics of Care*. Washington DC: Georgetown University Press.

Culliford L (2011) *The Psychology of Spirituality: An introduction*. London: Jessica Kingsley Publishers.

Davie G (1994) *Religion in Britain since 1945: Believing without belonging*. Oxford: Blackwell Publishers.

Department of Health (2012) *Compassion in Practice*. London: Department of Health.

Gilbert P (2011a) Understanding mental health and spirituality. In: Peter Gilbert (Ed) *Spirituality and Mental Health*. Brighton: Pavilion Publishing Ltd.

Gilbert P (2011b) Historical, spiritual and evolutionary approaches to suffering, compassion, caring and the caring professions. In Peter Gilbert (Ed) *Spirituality and Mental Health*. Brighton: Pavilion Publishing.

Gilbert P (2013) Between life and death. In Peter Gilbert (Ed) *Spirituality and End of Life Care*. Hove: Pavilion Publishing and Media Ltd.

Hayes M (2013) Nurturing goodness. *The Pastoral Review* **9** p5.

Stone B (1996) *Compassionate Ministry: Theological foundations*. Maryknoll, N.Y: Orbis Books.

Vernon M (2013) The prevalence of mental disorders among those who do God alone is an indictment of churches failure to meet their needs. *The Guardian*. Available at: http://theguardian.com/commentisfree/belief/2013/jan/09/spiritual-but-not-religious-dangerous-mix. (accessed November 2013).

Further reading

Armstrong K (2011) *Twelve Steps to a Compassionate Life*. London: The Bodley Head. This book offers a 12-step practical guide on how to live a compassionate life. It offers a multi-faith approach using examples from all the major world religions.

Ruffing J (1989) *Uncovering Stories of Faith*. Mahwah, NJ: Paulist Press. Chapter 4 contains a useful discussion of the connection between narrative, identity and meaning- making.

Fowler, James, W (1987) *Faith Development and Pastoral Care*. Philadephia: Fortress Press. Chapter 4 contains a useful account of Fowler's stages of faith development.

Chapter 9: Modelling well-being in social care

Hári Sewell

'Take time, enjoy the peacefulness of the grounds [Worth Abbey] or enjoy the chapel as a quiet place for reflection. We've built in time for you to be still or reflect however you choose. I'll be going for a run later. It's really important to take time to nurture ourselves. This is important time for us.' Peter Gilbert, on the 'down time' at the annual Social Care Strategic Network residential break.

Organisations that employ staff in the caring professions routinely state that staff are their most valuable resource. Often one of their corporate values relates to investing in the workforce. This is because it makes business sense as well as ethical sense. West *et al* (2012) draw a relationship between staff experience and the satisfaction and outcomes for people who use NHS services. There can be no more justifiable reason for investing in staff than improvements in outcomes for service users.

Peter could (and did) rationalise the investment in staff from the business perspective as well as any senior manager. He had run large departments in social care and knew what it meant to have the corporate performance of the department resting in the hands of the distributed workforce. Beyond the business arguments that conceptualise staff as resources, Peter saw people as people. This chapter explores the subject of well-being for leaders in social care and social workers, with particular reference to rest, reflection and restoration; aspects of the Social Care Strategic Network residentials that are valued by those who attend.

The Social Care Strategic Network (mental health) began life as a learning set for directors of social care or people in similar national roles. A key characteristic of the members was that they worked in integrated mental health settings, working at the interface of health and social care at a senior level. The learning set was started by two directors of social care and through support from the then National Institute for Mental Health England, Peter was brought in as the facilitator (see Gilbert, 2005, p42). Peter co-ordinated a group for staff at the next level down from the original senior group and then both merged and transmogrified in

2008 into a membership organisation called the Social Care Strategic Network (mental health).

A regular theme in the discussions at meetings was the aspects of these roles which related to mediating the tension between the NHS and the local authority, or on other occasions, advocating the social care agenda within medical (psychiatric) paradigms of problem solving, treatment and care. Members of the Network were aware that in their role working in a mental health trust (either substantively or through secondment) they needed also to demonstrate their corporate commitment. Being in roles that place social care workers in conflicting situations is not a unique position but this does not lessen the legitimacy in giving regard to the management of the consequences on those occupying such roles. The *Coaching at Work Toolkit* states that *'culture is a collectively shared strategy to prevent stress'* (Zeus & Skiffington, 2002, p54). Roles that straddle organisational culture and mediate between them will not benefit for that collectively shared strategy.

In many ways the director of social care type roles mirrored at a corporate level the tensions felt by staff at the frontline, working in multidisciplinary teams. In a study by Onyett *et al* (Sainsbury Centre for Mental Health, 1995), social workers ranked very low in the comparisons of job satisfaction, according to the disciplines that comprised community mental health teams (CMHTs) (Sainsbury Centre for Mental Health, 1995). Compared with other public sector professions, both adult and child care social workers face high levels of burnout and staff turnover (Social Work Task Force, 2009). The systemic challenges tackled by the Social Work Task Force are acknowledged. Alongside this, attention is given in this chapter to personal restoration.

Replenishment and leadership beyond dualistic ideas

The Francis Inquiry into the poor and devastating practices at Mid Staffordshire Hospital highlighted consequences of an organisational culture that pursued targets as if productivity and reflective ethical care were mutually exclusive (Francis, 2013). The book *NLP: The new technology of achievement* (1996), consistent with the title, defines NLP at the outset of the book as *'the study of human excellence'* (Andreas & Faulkner, 1996, p27). Towards the end of the book, in an appendix, Andreas and Faulkner urge readers to take time out for reflection and rest. It is perhaps the case that people in high powered jobs know intellectually that rest, reflection and restoration are important but do not manage to achieve this goal for themselves. The fallacy of being too busy to stop for rest or essential activity was highlighted in *The Seven Habits of Highly Effective People* (Covey, 1989) by use of an example of the tree cutter who was exhausted from sawing for five hours, but who greeted a suggestion that he rest and sharpen the saw, with a retort that he was too busy sawing to stop. There is a binary notion that people are either busy or alternatively they have time for a break. This is one example of binary thinking that can be detected in the language of health and social care managers and frontline staff who almost boast that they are too busy to stop for lunch. Such a fragmented view of the world is also detected in beliefs about intellectual intelligence, spirituality and the loci of decision-making intelligence in organisations.

Fostering emotional intelligence

Daniel Goleman's *Emotional Intelligence* (1995) sets out the case for a new understanding about the abilities that it takes to manage and lead. He explores the hitherto privilege given intellect: *'What factors are at play when people with high IQ founder and those with modest IQ do surprisingly well? I would argue that the differences often lie in the abilities called here emotional intelligence, which include self-control, zeal and persistence, and the ability to motivate one's self'* (Goleman, 1995, pxii). Goleman goes on to talk about the need for self-reflection as a means to developing emotional intelligence. Peter provided a solid example of when emotional intelligence was a defining factor in a change programme that had previously stalled. In a section of his book on effective leadership headed 'Achieving results', Peter describes the process of engaging trade unions, service users and carers, and other key stakeholders in arrangements to outsource home care services in Worcester (Gilbert, 2005). Changing the persistence of views about a hardnosed management style being essential for the achievement of results as opposed to more emotional intelligence, Peter states that *'Such involvement is not some kind of soft option, it is an essential part of the process'* (Gilbert, 2005, p90). This was in reference to the engagement of stakeholders in the project to outsource home care. This emotional intelligence is in part a product of self-reflection and awareness.

Fostering inclusive decision making

The Worcester illustration acknowledges that decision-making expertise is not the preserve of a chosen few. Kline (1999) states that *'Organisations also intimidate people into believing that "the higher up you are in the hierarchy, the better you can think"'* (p59). In *The Professional Decision Thinker* (Heirs, 1986) the premise is set that executives are employed to think, but then it goes on to state that this executive thinking is at its best when thinking teams are created.

Peter was mindful of the fact that the interaction between role pressures and personal styles could lead to managers pursing job goals in a single-minded way at the exclusion of engagement. He saw it as a real gift to provide a time and an environment at the residentials for self-reflection, rest and restoration so that even the most gifted intellectuals could become even more effective leaders.

Fostering integrated Ideas of well-being

Descartes, the French philosopher (1596–1650), is widely acknowledged as establishing the common understanding of the distinction between mind and body. Consequentially referred to as Cartesian dualism, this idea is problematic in creating a distinction that obscures the reality of how we function (Bracken & Thomas, 2005). Academics and managers in the field of human resources management map relationships between workplace pressures and sickness absence, noting that physical ailments arise from emotional stress. Peter encouraged reflective time based on his integrated models of people. He encouraged rest not just of the physical form including the brain, which would be exhausted from insufficient rest and down time (in an immediate sense), but also the mind in terms of patterns of thinking. It is worth noting the paradox that this kind of rest, reflection and restoration is an active process. The concept of sharpening the saw is active (Covey, 1989). Peter's personal approach to de-cluttering his mind included road running. The mind and the body are not distinct. Recuperation does not necessarily mean rest. Just as organisational thinking is not a discrete activity of a select few, rest and recuperation cannot validly be seen as an immediate response to physical fatigue. More integrative approaches are needed.

Spirituality

'Every world religion and spiritual discipline has times of rest' (Andreas & Faulkner, 1996, p312). This reference in *NLP: The new technology of achievement* (Andreas & Faulkner, 1996) reflects the integration of another binary distinction, which is unhelpful and which Peter did much to address. This is the distinction between secularism and religiosity. Peter led national work for the Department of Health on spirituality. The quote from Peter at the beginning of this chapter illustrates the way in which he integrated the secular with the religious for the purposes of supporting the well-being of colleagues. The choice of venue was not based purely on commercial or travel needs. Worth Abbey was chosen because, using his personal connections, Peter was able to secure an environment where stillness and reflection was the norm. In his book on leadership, Peter describes aspects of holistic personal well-being and in this section he refers to spiritual

needs as *'recommitting to core values; meditation and contemplation; relaxation; exploration of "being" and "becoming"'* (Gilbert, 2005, p41). These elements are not religious in the traditional sense. In *Emotional Intelligence* (1995), Goleman begins his chapter on self-awareness by referencing religious concepts, which he then develops his arguments based on his expertise in psychology. Feifel (1958, p565) states *'In Hinduism, for instance, psychology and religion are the same subject and have always been so'*. The Sunday Assembly movement creates godless congregations to celebrate life and represents an integration of Christian religious practices (Sunday gathering and a determination to do good) with a secular position (no deity, no doctrine).

The strengths of a non-dualistic view of religion and secularism are that they take the valuable aspects of different walks of life and practice inclusivity. On the Social Care Strategic Network residential breaks when Peter encouraged colleagues to use the chapels he was explicit that this was not a call to faith but that they could use the reflective space in a way that made sense to them. The alternative of just enjoying the grounds, the stillness, the fresh air and lush vegetation was another sign of inclusivity, catering for different preferences.

Inclusivity and diversity

Leaders in social care must model behaviours. Policies and edicts about diversity and inclusivity will not suffice (Sewell, 2009). Goleman (1995) states: *'the sad fact is that the panoply of one-day, one-video, or single weekend "diversity training" courses do not really seem to budge the biases of those employees who come to them with deep prejudice...'* (p156). Goleman states that prejudices begin at an emotional level. It is through self-awareness that appreciation for others can develop (Gilbert, 2005; Goleman, 1995).

'Diversity raises the intelligence of groups ... diversity enhances thinking because it is true ... the mind works best in the presence of reality ... conversely, the mind seems to lose its edge when having to work in pretence, denial or fabrication ... And homogeneity, when you think about it, is a form of denial. It is a form of pretence.' (Kline, 1999, p87).

Taking time for rest, reflection and restoration it seems is not a luxury which can only be afforded in idealised conditions but is critical for successful leadership and management. The consequences for self of not doing so are potential burnout and loss of valuable contributions. The consequences for staff in the organisation are poor leadership and weak culture and values. The consequences for service users relate to care where empathy is sublimated to other drivers for behaviour, usually relating to productivity, performance management or personal preservation of workers.

Serving on the front line: social workers and well-being

Relationship-Based Social Work (Ruch *et al*, 2010) sets out understandings of social work practice, which include: '*A collaborative relationship is the means through which interventions are channelled, and this requires a particular emphasis to be placed on the use of self*' (p21). As the book points out, the use of self requires self-awareness (drawing on psychoanalytic principles) because past experiences and emotions will unconsciously, as well as consciously, impact on relationships with service users. Gilbert *et al* (2010) in describing self-management includes the call to social workers to build personal resilience and to avoid becoming over-stressed. Given the findings about stress, staff turnover and absence reported by the Social Work Task Force (2009), it appears that the profession itself and social work organisations have some way to go in prioritising well-being.

The Francis Inquiry (Francis, 2013) has placed compassion centre-stage in the NHS, but in health and social care services more generally. Goleman states '*Empathy builds on self-awareness; the more open we are to our own emotions, the more skilled we will be in reading feelings*' (p96). Mirroring the important elements described in this chapter, Goossen (2013) discusses how social workers gain satisfaction in their compassion; employing reflection, and physical, psychological, emotional, spiritual and professional self-care strategies. The considerations of the centrality of relationships in social work highlight the emphasis on the relationship between self-reflection and self-awareness; the relationship between self-awareness and empathy and the relationship between these activities and rest, reflection and restoration. Further, ideas about leadership as modelling the behaviours that are valued, and the creation of thinking teams and spaces, emphasise how important it is that leaders model good personal well-being.

Conclusion

The annual Social Care Strategic Network residential breaks continue to run. With less than a month away from the 2013 event, Peter Gilbert was in a hospice. It marked a full year since he first received his diagnosis. It is 10 years since Peter began facilitating the learning set which became the Network. There are many colleagues who have benefited from the rest, reflection and restoration of the residentials. There have been a few occasions at residentials where Peter worked on final edits of articles that he had co-authored with colleagues who never considered themselves to be academic or writers. Embedded within the culture of the Network is the priority given to well-being. There are no metrics, no performance management, no top-down imperatives but each year colleagues return, describing how disciplined they needed to be to preserve the time. In essence, that is a key performance indicator and in recognition of Peter's influence, a powerful legacy.

References

Andreas S & Faulkner C (1996) *NLP: The New Technology of Achievement*. London: Nicholas Brealy Publishing.

Bracken P & Thomas P (2005) Postpsychiatry: *Mental Health in a Postmodern World: International perspectives in philosophy and psychiatry*. Oxford: Oxford University Press.

Covey S (1989) *The 7 Habits of Highly Effective People: Powerful Lessons in Personal Change*. New York: Fireside.

Feifel H (1958) Symposium on relationships between religion and mental health: introductory remarks. *American Psychologist* **13** (10) 565–566.

Francis R (2013) *Report of the Mid Staffordshire NHS Foundation Trust Public Inquiry*. London: Crown.

Gilbert P (2005) *Leadership: Being effective and remaining human*. Dorset: Russell House Publishing.

Gilbert P, Bates P, Carr S, Clark M, Gould N & Slay G (2010) *Social Work and Mental Health: The value of everything*. Dorset: Russell House Publishing.

Goleman D (1995) *Emotional Intelligence: Why it can matter more than IQ*. London: Bloomsbury.

Goossen L (2013) Happy days. *Social Work Matters*, February, p24–28. London: College of Social Work.

Heirs B (1986) *The Professional Decision Thinker: Our new management priority*. London: Sidgwick & Jackson Ltd.

Kline N (1999) *Time to Think: Listening to ignite the human mind*. London: Ward Lock.

Ruch G, Turney D & Ward A (2010) *Relationship-Based Social Work: Getting to the heart of practice*. London: Jessica Kingsley Publishers.

Sainsbury Centre for Mental Health (1995) *Making Community Mental Health Teams Work: CMHTs and the people who work in them*. London: SCMH.

Sewell H (2009) Leading race equality in mental health. *International Journal of Leadership in Public Services* **5** (2) 19–16.

Social Work Task Force (2009) *Facing Up to the Task: The interim report of the social work task force*. London: Department of Health & Department for Children, Schools and Families.

West M, Dawson J, Admasachew L & Topakas A (2012) NHS Staff Management and Health Service Quality. Available at: https://www.gov.uk/government/uploads/system/uploads/attachment_data/file/215455/dh_129656.pdf (accessed January 2014).

Zeus P & Skiffington S (2002) *The Coaching at Work Toolkit: A complete guide to techniques and practices*. Sydney: McGraw-Hill.

Further resources

The Sunday Assembly: www.sundayassembly.com

Spirituality and interfaith relations

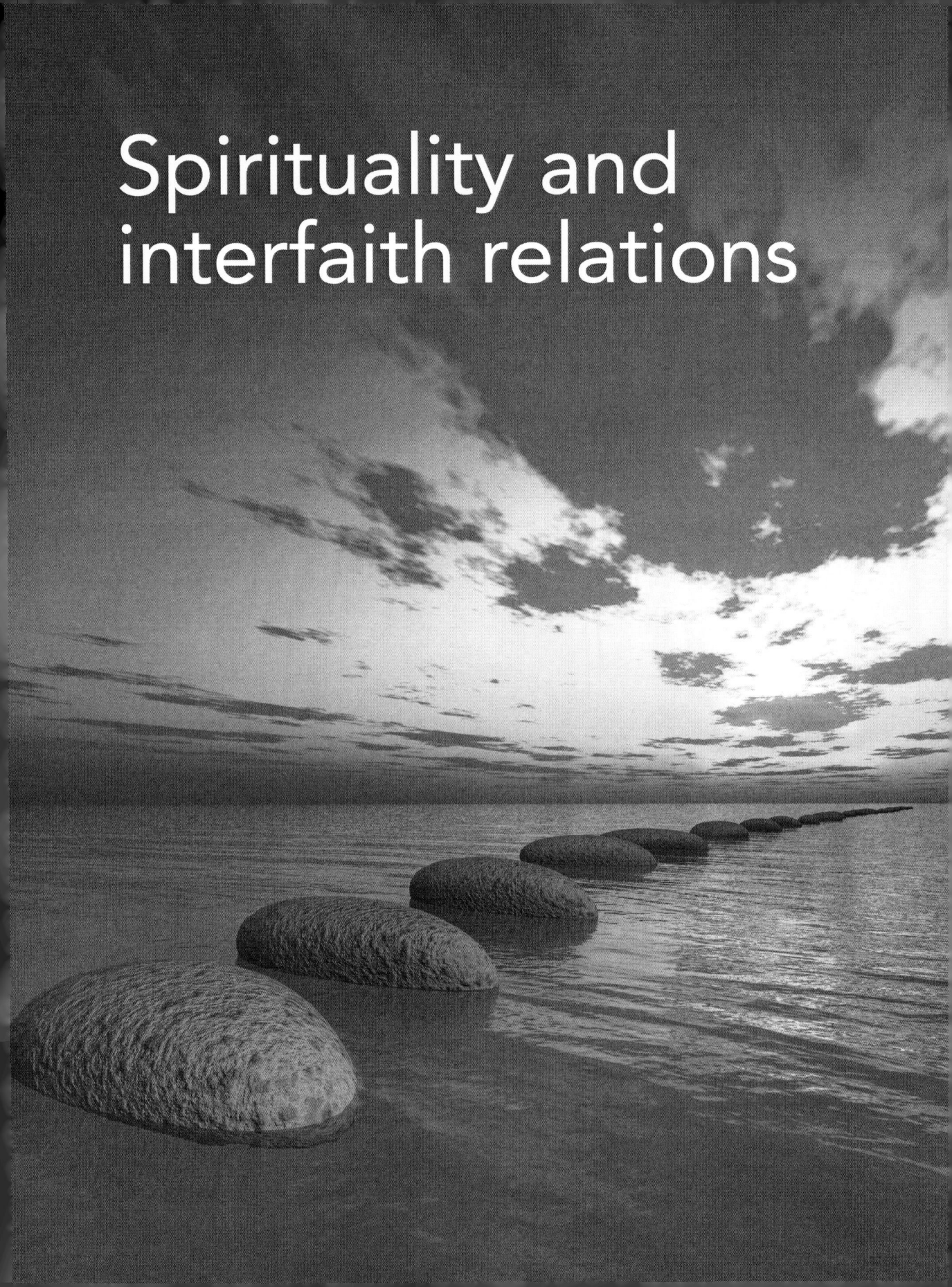

Chapter 10: The Gilbert pilgrimage

Martin Aaron

Human beings live usually by virtue of believing and belonging together. The relationship of a child with its mother is the fundamental primordial tie in human life, and considered the blueprint for the child's future relationships. Besides this initial bond, we all begin our lives as part of a cultural family, we learn its beliefs, its faith, fears, strengths and weaknesses, and thereby become connected to its ethnic consciousness. Our spirituality motivates and vitalises us, and belonging to a family is the central bond that unites us with its members, but through which it connects us with friends and other groups. It is due to these connections that we become mindful of the importance of inclusion and sharing with others outside our own family group, and we come to realise how painful it can be to be excluded by others.

There are not many people in our lives who have made a difference to us and to other people. Peter Gilbert was one of those exceptional individuals who embodied the rich diversity of the human spirit and the humanity with which he conveyed it to those around him. Peter was an excellent communicator, he combined his knowledge and skills in every delivery with precision and great attention to detail. He was an excellent strategist and as a planner, purposeful in his objectives. He was a born leader. Our troubled world is in dire need of more people like Peter.

The beginnings of the National Spirituality and Mental Health Forum

In the first half of the 1990s a Judeo-Christian advisory group was formed under the auspices of the former Health Education Authority (HEA) and I became the Jewish representative on the group. Its purpose was to establish to what degree the clergy of the two faiths understood mental illness, and how they would react and deal with the problem if confronted with mental illness among members of their communities.

I first met Peter towards the end of the 1990s when he first attended the working group meetings held at the HEA under the chair of Dr Lynne Friedli. This was just prior to the HEA's closure by the Department of Health at the start of 2000. Following this, the group was renamed the Spirituality Forum and transferred to Mentality, a charity which became part of the Sainsbury Centre for Mental Health. The Centre acted as the Forum's secretariat for two years. As attendees from various faith groups joined, it very soon became known as a multifaith and interfaith forum. Peter attended regularly, spoke at several meetings and made a significant contribution to the Forum's growth, particularly in its interfaith work.

After I had taken over as chair of the Forum at the start of 2003, and with the support of the Department of Health, I registered the Forum as an independent, national, multifaith charity with the title of The National Spirituality and Mental Health Forum. The members of the board of trustees constitute representatives of all nine religions recognised by the Department of Health: Baha'i, Buddhism, Christianity, Hinduism, Islam, Jainism, Judaism, Sikhism, Zoroastrianism and humanists, together with representatives of no particular religious affiliation it soon became an exciting and formidable force of likeminded people, all determined to promote the importance of spirituality in the lives of everyone.

The Forum meets at least four times a year in open meetings. It has as its main objective the establishment of ongoing discussion, interaction and joint working among all people, so as to ensure that spirituality is well understood as the main component in all our lives, irrespective of whether one is a religious person or not.

The impact of 9/11: a changing world and the Spirituality Project

In 2001, the United Nations declared a 'Year of Dialogue between Civilizations' and in that very year there followed the horrific tragedy of 9/11. Peter often referred to the tragedy in his work and in the many papers he presented. At an opening meeting of the National Forum in 2007 he stated: *'Every so often an event occurs that utterly changes people's view of the world. The tragic event on September the 11th, 2001, with its triple assault on the pillars of Western capitalism – the World Trade Center (finance and commerce), the Pentagon (industrial–military complex) and the White House (global politics) – was one of those markers in the sand.'*

Our lives are indeed affected by the environment within which we live and events such as 9/11 most certainly brought about certain changes in views.

With the expected backlash towards Muslim communities as a result of 9/11, Peter and Anthony Sheehan, group head of mental health at the Department of Health, immediately launched the interfaith 'Spirituality Project' in the NHS with the object of conveying the importance of spiritual care in the health service, inviting all ethnic and religious groups to participate in the multifaith and interfaith project.

Peter declared that the aim of the Project was to inspire hope and *'to collate current thinking on the importance of spirituality in mental health on an individual and group basis, to evaluate the role of faith communities in the field of mental health and to develop and promote good practice in the whole person approach'* (Gilbert & Nicholls, 2003).

Recognising the importance of spirituality in the whole person approach to mental health, Peter became the prime mover in the project. In November 2003 he was instrumental in launching a two-year project partnership between The National Institute for Mental Health in England (NIMHE) and the Mental Health Foundation. This partnership was to further ensure the bringing together of all faiths and beliefs to develop current thinking and practice in the area of spirituality and mental health. As a result of Peter's positive thinking, determination and skill, the partnership was a great success.

Bumps in the road for the Spirituality Project

With the growing membership of the Forum, Peter and I, together with our Forum colleagues, felt that it was essential to form a link between the NHS Spirituality Project and the National Forum. The partnership between us was to prove its worth from the commencement of the Project in 2001 until the Department of Health decided to terminate it due to the reduction in government funding at the end of March 2008. This was a great disappointment to the Forum, and particularly to Peter who had put his heart and soul into the project, and invested so much of his time in it.

Peter and his colleagues all felt that the professional and social capital built up by the project through his work in the NHS as a result of the Department of Health's initial investment in the project, would be wasted, to a major degree, if the Project's funding was discontinued. As Peter stated at the time, the important contacts and interaction between members of all faiths, both service providers in the NHS, outside agencies, as well as the important service users, would be weakened, if not lost altogether. It is well-known that the NHS is continually going through periods of change, often frustrating staff, who move on to pastures new. The movement of staff often severs the important link which anchor personnel, who are so important to the ongoing implementation of a project and its training.

All felt that the negative response from the Department of Health was totally out of line with the declared statements of its former Secretary of State Alan Johnson who had declared that the essential compassion had been lost in the NHS.

Peter, committed to the continual promotion of interfaith spirituality, particularly with his work in the health service, continued to maintain the numerous contacts which he had made with all faiths through the Project on a pro bono basis; such was his dedication to his work. He did this while the Forum, having made an application for funding to the Department of Health, awaited the result in order to continue the project in the NHS. All of Peter's colleagues and associates agree that his life's journey was like a pilgrimage, with him carrying the 'spirituality banner' into whichever venue or area of the country he worked.

Fortunately, a year later the Forum was successful in obtaining a three-year grant for the Project, but which sadly terminated at the end of March 2012.

The Forum's interfaith work

The interfaith work of the Forum is an essential component in good relationships in the UK's multifaith society; it brings members of all faiths, beliefs and those of no faith together in a continual dialogue, particularly on health issues. On many occasions speakers from different ethnic, cultural and religious backgrounds have made presentations at Forum open meetings, seminars and conferences. Many speakers have highlighted the significance of their religion or faith, but each commenting on their common belief in one creator.

During past millennia various cultures, institutions and religions have evolved, and throughout the centuries, prophets, disciples, sages, saints and teachers have taught the peoples of this world. The word 'spirituality' is fairly new in the world's languages. In Judaism it derives from the word 'ru'ach', meaning 'spirit', contained in the second sentence in the opening chapter of Genesis in the Old Testament, concerning the creation in which it records *and the spirit of God hovered over the face of the waters'*.

The mystery attached to the Creator has been richly expressed by numerous writers past and present in many different ways and also the relationship between God and man, and God and religion. One prolific writer often referred to by Peter is the former chief rabbi, professor Lord Jonathan Sacks. In the first edition of his book *The Dignity of Difference* (2002), Sacks states: *'The radical transcendence of God in the Hebrew Bible means nothing more or less than there is a difference between God and religion. God is universal, religion is particular ... In the course of history, God has spoken to mankind in many languages through Judaism to Jews, Christianity to Christians, Islam to Muslims ... In heaven there is truth; on earth there are truths. Therefore, each culture has something to contribute.'*

Every human being must be free to choose their faith or belief, while paying respect to all others.

Inclusiveness and unity

Inclusiveness was an important part of Peter's drive for the equality of all people, irrespective of their faith, belief, ethnic background or disability. He was dedicated to the cause of equality and chaired the National Development Team for Inclusion for some years. In his article 'Integrating a spirited dimension into health and social care', Peter argues that the place of individual spirituality and religious faith is increasingly being recognised by the NHS and other organisations (Gilbert, 2010). During the last few years this has most certainly been the case with demands that much closer attention be given to patients' ethnic and cultural background as recipients of both health and social care. Besides medication and therapeutic services, people want services that treat them as a whole person, in their whole environment. Peter *believed* that services need *'to tap into people's inner resources, their sense of identity, meaning and purpose – their spirituality – so as to combine effectiveness, humanity, dignity and cost effectiveness'* (Gilbert, 2010).

Religious diversity and social unity are important components of society today. In our everyday life we are dependent upon others to support and sustain us, and similarly they are dependent on us. We all have need for one another. Rowan Williams, the previous Archbishop of Canterbury, made reference to the importance of diversity and unity in his recent book *Faith in the Public Square* (2012), in which he concluded: *'I would maintain that the presence of diverse religious groups in a society, allowed to have a voice in the decision-making processes of society without embarrassment, is potentially an immense contribution to a genuinely active and inter-active social harmony and a sense of moral accountability within the social order.'*

As Peter so often advocated, spirituality is at the very heart of our covenant with people of all faiths and beliefs, and with those of no particular religion. We all emanate from the same moral community and while we accept its trust, we ourselves entrust ourselves to it. For too many years now we have witnessed the decline in family values. Many family units have broken up due to the lack of interaction between parents and their children. Rarely do families sit together over a meal and discuss what's happening in each other's lives and in the environment around them. Certainly, in most faiths the family unit is, or has been, at the core of its moral survival, and each family of whichever religion has an enduring social covenant of responsibility not only for its own individual members, but for all others.

'To be in covenant with other people involves believing that we and they belong to the same moral community; that in this community each person matters in his and her own right and not merely as something useful to the society; that we all participate in the moral community by entrusting ourselves to others and in turn by accepting their entrusting; and that in the moral community each of us has an enduring responsibility to all the others.' (Allen, 1995)

Through Peter's work and that of The National Spirituality and Mental Health Forum, new friends and relationships have been formed between members of different faiths and beliefs. It is most gratifying to know that many are supporting one another in times of need, and have formed local groups in the UK.

Empathy and compassion

In conclusion, to be a responsible member of a responsible society, we have to commit ourselves to being at all times mindful of others. We have to understand another person's emotions, to sense and respond appropriately in their solitude to their feelings and concerns. Being able to sense what another person feels is at the core of a person's empathy and compassion, which are two of the most important elements in hospital and social care.

In order to carry these essential principles through, we have to understand ourselves. Who am I? What am I doing here? What am I supposed to be doing here? The primary purpose of life is undoubtedly to know oneself. We cannot do so unless we can identify ourselves with all who live around us. We must conform with a moral code and help in creating a society based on compassion and respect for human dignity. Peter, who had been a service user himself, well understood what it was like being both on the delivery end, as well as the receiving end of health and care services.

Irrespective of the community or faith into which we were born, the sense of belonging, love and compassion are the essentials of our life's existence. It is true that for some people, conflicting forces within them – our inner egotistic tendencies on the one hand and the altruistic tendencies on the other – may make the process of our bonding with others a somewhat difficult task. However, the degree of integration finally achieved will, to a major degree, depend upon the balance we create between these opposing elements.

I cannot believe that in any divine plan human beings should be working in opposition to one another. Surely a person with an open mind, who cultivates the greatest qualities of his or her own ethnic culture and its principles, will acquire knowledge and insight into other faiths and cultures. In so doing, they will benefit all mankind as national culture can act as a bridge, not an obstacle, to mutual intellectual and spiritual understanding.

In *Group Psychology and the Analysis of the Ego* (1922), Freud states that *'in the development of mankind as a whole, just as in individuals, love alone acts as a civilizing factor in the sense that it brings a change from egoism to altruism'*. Here, then, lies the task of the educator, religious leader, psychiatrist, and presenter of the spiritual dimension, which was so much a part of Peter's life.

I hope that the future will bring about a greater understanding of the other, through a more adequate, more realistic relationship between members of all faiths and beliefs, and those of no faith in a world in which we may all live peaceably together.

I feel privileged to have been asked to contribute to this work in recognition of the important part my colleague and friend professor Peter Gilbert played, particularly over the past 15 years that I knew him, in promoting the essential role of spirituality in all our lives. Those who worked with him were aware of his dedication to the common humanity of all people, irrespective of race, religion or culture. He was a compassionate man whose vocation in life was in the service of others.

References

Allen J (1995) *Love and Conflict: A covenantal model of Christian ethics*. Lanham, MD: University Press of America.

Freud S (1922) *Group Psychology and the Analysis of the Ego*. New York: Bond and Liveright.

Gilbert P (2010) Integrating a spirited dimension into health and social care. *The British Journal of Well-Being* **1** (3) 20–24.

Gilbert P & Nicholls V (2003) *Inspiring Hope: Recognising the importance of spirituality in a whole person approach*. London: DH/MHF.

Sacks J (2002) *The Dignity of Difference*. London: Continuum Books.

Williams R (2012) *Faith in the Public Square*. London: Bloomsbury Publishing PLC.

Chapter 11: Dying to live: graduating from the University of Life

Chetna Kang

Hinduism and death

I first met Peter at Bhaktivedanta Manor on Janamastami in 2005 – one of the biggest Hindu festivals of the year which celebrates the appearance of Lord Krishna. We had arranged to meet there to discuss the upcoming Spirituality and Mental Health Symposium to be held at Staffordshire University. In his usual style he wanted to dive right in, immerse himself in the festivities and get firsthand experience of what many of the other 65,000 pilgrims had come for. It just so happened that our very first conversation was exactly about the topic of this book. Peter was always hungry to hear about the different faith perspectives and we had an enthusiastic discussion about how the Hindu faith sees death as an opportunity to graduate from the University of Life. Who or what is dying? And what possibilities await us? It was here that our ongoing discussions about how life is a preparation for death first began.

Although Hinduism is an umbrella term for a number of spiritual paths largely practised in India, all of them stem from the Vedas, hence all are governed by the same core principles. The Vedas are said to have been written down 5,000 years ago and passed down orally prior to this. They are an immense body of knowledge covering topics including, but not limited to, mathematics, medicine, cosmology and architecture. However, the majority of the texts, and in particular the Bhagavad Gita and Srimad Bhagavatam, discuss the science of the self, the individual's relationship with God and how to use our current lifetime to prepare for its end and a new beginning. Hindus usually refer to God by one of his many, many names. So, in keeping with what is natural to me I will be referring to God as Krishna.

The science of the self

'As the embodied soul continuously passes, in this body, from boyhood to youth to old age, the soul similarly passes into another body at death. A sober person is not bewildered by such a change. For the soul there is neither birth nor death at any time.' (Bhagavad Gita 2.13)

Every journey must begin with knowledge of our starting point. To this end, an understanding of what makes up the 'self' is crucial for any Hindu. The Vedic paradigm describes that every individual is made up of the temporary and transient self, which is said to be the body and the mind, and the permanent self otherwise known as the soul. The body and mind are subjected to and affected by birth, disease, old age and death and are seen as an outer covering or vehicle for the soul while we are here. The happiness that is experienced here is said to be a shadow of spiritual happiness and more like the absence of suffering, such as food only being pleasurable when one is hungry. The soul on the other hand is not influenced by time or loss and gain in the material sense. The soul or 'we' are said to be inherently eternal, full in wisdom and ever blissful. The soul and body/mind are compared to a bird in a cage. To experience deep, long lasting happiness, simply looking after the cage will not be sufficient, the bird also needs feeding. The practices of hearing from or reading scripture, chanting or meditating on Krishna's names, prayer, deity worship and associating with saintly persons are considered 'soul food'. As the soul becomes nourished, our constitutional identity comes to the forefront and as the temporary designations placed on us by our psychophysical nature move to the background, one can see everything for what it actually is and experience a happiness that is not dependent on external circumstances or the whims of the mind.

However, the Vedas emphasise that the body and mind are not to be neglected as they house the soul and until self-realisation is achieved they are our vehicle to express our love and service to Krishna and society. The laws of karma (action) and reincarnation reinforce that the body/mind and its experiences are temporary and are not to be mistaken for the real self. The laws of karma dictate that as we sow, so we shall reap. Instilling accountability and ownership of one's own desires, thoughts and actions. The laws of reincarnation state that *'whatever state one remembers at the time of death, that state he shall attain in the next life. One who remembers Me (Krishna) returns to me'* (Bhagavad Gita 8.5–6). We are most likely to think of that which we are most attached to at the time of death and this attachment is likely to be the result of many desires and activities pertaining to it; life itself is in its entirety, a preparation for either the individual soul being yet again subjected to another temporary body or achieving permanent freedom from birth and death and regaining their place with Krishna. The relationship between us and Krishna is said not only to be an eternal one, but one which is based on love, which by definition requires that we use our free will to choose to re-establish the connection.

Other than the promise of eternal happiness, why desire to return to the Kingdom of God? The answer lies in the unfoldment of our true identity. Just as our identities here are relative to something and more often to someone (I am a mother, a sister, a teacher, a sweeper), so equally, the Vedas suggest that our true and eternal identities fully manifest themselves when in relationship with Krishna, which can happen in life as well as after death.

Our relationship with Krishna

'One can understand Me as I am, as the Supreme Personality of Godhead, only by devotional service. And when one is in full consciousness of Me by such devotion, he can enter into the kingdom of God.' (Bhagavad Gita 18.55)

Said to have originated from Krishna, the Vedas go into great detail about the various ways in which one can relate to Krishna depending on what an individual is ready for.

Seeing Krishna's presence through nature: The Universal form, or 'Virat Rupa' as it is otherwise known, is a way of conceptualising Krishna by seeing His majesty in nature and is a popular first step to relating to Him.

Connecting with Krishna as an energy or higher force: This is known as the 'Brahmajyoti'. Many who take this approach are aiming to achieve a state of 'moksa' or freedom from birth and death by merging into Krishna's energy and light.

'Paramatma' or Supersoul: This is the form of Krishna that alongside the individual soul is said to reside in every living entity's heart. In meditating on this aspect of Krishna, one receives realisation of Virat Rupa and Brahmajyoti but also a somewhat more personal experience of Krishna.

Connecting to Krishna the person through 'Bhakti' (love and devotion): This is said to be the ultimate level of relationship with Him. Whereas the preceding approaches do bring spiritual happiness, it is coming from a place of awe and reverence; whereas with Bhakti the devotee experiences a spiritual happiness which is rooted in love and surrender where Krishna, overcome by the love of His devotee, eventually takes the position of the servant and allows us to become

His master. This is said to be the most organic way for a practitioner to grow spiritually as the need to be loved and give love are innate in everyone and it is very difficult to have affection for an abstract concept of Krishna.

Crossing over to the riverbank of love

'One who is not envious but is a kind friend to all living entities, who does not think himself a proprietor and is free from false ego, who is equal in both happiness and distress, who is tolerant, always satisfied, self-controlled, and engaged in devotional service with determination, his mind and intelligence fixed on Me – such a devotee of Mine is very dear to Me.' (Bhagavad Gita 12.13–14)

Developing a stronger attraction for Krishna than the people and objects of this world has its challenges. Living in this world but knowing that we are not of this world is equally challenging. Some of the obstacles include, as is common to many faiths; lust (this does not just refer to sexual desire but also the desire to enjoy anything just for ourselves), greed, anger, envy, illusion (particularly the illusion of thinking we are nothing more than this body) and madness (living a life based solely on a temporary sense of self is seen as madness and this is not a reference to mental illness). Another obstacle that is frequently emphasised is 'Ahankara' or false ego. This is essentially the sense of 'I' and 'mine' in relationship to our current psychosociophysical make up and the stronger this is the more likely we are to succumb to pride and arrogance. However, these qualities are part of our human nature and not our spiritual nature, which is compassionate, merciful, selfless, kind and truthful. So rather than ignoring the obstacles, one practises not succumbing to them and simultaneously nourishing the spiritual nature, so that our divine qualities come through.

Our human side also has a lot to offer this world, and rather than seeing it as an obstacle, the Vedas advise that we understand our particular vehicle both psychically and psychologically, and engage in work or activity that is befitting, makes a positive contribution to society in a manner and with the motive to please Krishna. This type of action is accepted by Krishna as an offering of love and instead of binding us here, increases our attachment to Him. Thus, one can live in this world but with the consciousness that we are not of this world.

Spiritual progress in contrast to material progress is said to never be lost and any evolution of consciousness is carried over if we do return and take another body here. Some say that a manifestation of this is the varying degrees to which we are born with an attraction to spirituality even in the same families. What is most reassuring is that no matter how long we take to exercise our free will, to once and for all let this world go and cross the river, Krishna is patiently waiting for us on the other side, at the Riverbank of Love. Peter, I know, found great comfort in this.

'O Govinda! Feeling Your separation, I am considering a moment to be like 12 years or more. Tears are flowing from my eyes like torrents of rain, and I am feeling all vacant in the world in Your absence.

I know no one but Krishna as my Lord, and He shall remain so even if He handles me roughly by His embrace or makes me brokenhearted by not being present before me. He is completely free to do anything and everything, for He is always my worshipful Lord unconditionally.'

(Verses 7 & 8 from Sri Siksastakam by Caitanya Mahaprabhu 1486–1535)

Chapter 12: Spirituality, Buddhism and psychological therapies – a perspective

Sarajane Aris

'The way is not in the sky. The way is in the heart.' Lama Zopa Rinpoche

Introduction

Compassion and wisdom are at the heart of Buddhist practice and the path to awakening. The majority of spiritual traditions include the importance of love and compassion, the expression of our Buddha or True Nature. This is an essential quality that Peter strove to embody. He was embracing and inclusive of all people he came into contact with, and in particular the users of mental health services. It seems fitting to include a chapter that speaks to his essential and true nature.

This chapter is divided into sections that briefly outline some key cornerstones of Buddhism, including a section on death and dying, which is so essential to the heart of Buddhism. This outline sets a context for a final summary looking at how aspects of Buddhism have been applied in other contexts. In this case our focus is on key psychological therapies that have incorporated aspects of Buddhism and a spiritual perspective, in particular compassion in compassion-focused therapy. Throughout the chapter there are some reflective exercises to help the reader connect more directly with the content.

Cornerstones of Buddhism

This section will offer a very brief introduction to particular cornerstones of Buddhism relevant to themes of this chapter, namely:

- the Four Noble Truths
- Buddha or True Nature,
- compassion, the heart and path of our True Nature
- awareness and the path of awakening
- relative and absolute truth.

For Buddha, the journey to awakening began with questions about truth, suffering, the nature of suffering, how we can end that suffering, not just in this life, but in all future lives, not just for oneself, but for all beings, and how we can prepare for death. This is referred to as the 'Four Noble Truths'. It is more often than not the death or impending death of our loved ones, or facing death ourselves, that throws up and brings into focus questions about 'who and what suffers; who or what dies' and issues about our impermanence. This life that we grasp onto as real is impermanent and ends with death, so we need to let go of attachment in order to find what is of undying worth – the ungraspable mysterious essence of our being – our True Nature – sometimes referred to as 'Buddha nature'. This is present and accessible to us right now; it is what is ultimately real. However, in our daily lives we are often so caught up with what we are doing that this obscures our ability to connect with our True Nature. It is like the sun and the clouds; the sun is always shining, but its light is obscured by the clouds. Sometimes we get a sense of our essence or True Nature when someone we love and are close to dies – we feel them living on in our hearts and a deep sense of connectedness. That felt sense is more than just a memory – it is a deeper, all-encompassing way of knowing, beyond thinking and our everyday self. This relates to Peter's often posed question, 'What makes us tick?'

How do we connect with that deeper part of ourselves, the part that 'makes us tick', that part of us that really knows? From a Buddhist perspective, that sense of connectedness and way of knowing is reached by connecting with and developing our wisdom and compassion, through cultivating awareness, meditation practices, and by following the Buddhist teachings and path. When we find this other way of knowing, this living force, already accessible to us in the depth of our being and hearts, we can begin to see what is possible to know about the true nature of life and death. This is the path of awakening reached through the practice of meditation and compassion.

Opening our compassionate heart with compassion itself can therefore reveal to us what is unchanging in our nature – our Essence or True Nature, a timeless reality that is not born and does not die – we need to have confidence in this.

The practices of mindfulness, meditation, and specific practices that develop our compassion (Gilbert, 2011) can also help us develop this confidence. Before his illness, Peter took regular retreats in order to give himself space to connect with his True Nature.

Compassion in Tibetan Buddhism is often referred to as the 'wish-fulfilling jewel' (Rinpoche, 1992). It is seen as the source and essence of who we are, of enlightenment and the heart of enlightened activity – if we can be truly selfless, seeing others' needs as more important than our own, we are acting from a place of deep or 'great compassion'. This can be hard for us to do, until we have developed self-compassion (Neff, 2011). Compassion helps us to work with and transform our suffering and the suffering of others on the path. The more in touch we are with our compassion, the more in touch we are with our True Nature. The more we are in touch with ourselves and our True Nature, the more compassionate we become. The power of compassion has no bounds. Compassion is often referred to as 'Bodhichitta' – loving-kindness or 'the heart of the Enlightened Mind'.

'The water of compassion courses through the canal of loving-kindness.' (Buddha Maitraya).

We can learn to both awaken and develop our compassion in many ways. There are a number of Tibetan Buddhist teachings and practices specifically related to developing compassion. These are beyond the scope of this chapter. (For further information please refer to the appendices where they are listed and the references provided at the end of the chapter.)

Reflective exercise

Spend a moment settling yourself in your own way; remember a person or experience that for you represents love and compassion. Evoke a sense of this in your being and body, and see what arises in your heart. Stay with this for a short while. If any images, thoughts or feelings arise, make a note of them. Perhaps put a hand on your heart, and see if this touches anything within you.

As your heart opens, let love flow from it, extending it to all beings. Begin with those closest to you, then extend your love to your friends, acquaintances, neighbours, strangers, to those who you have difficulty with, and finally to the whole universe. Let your love feel boundless. This practice can inspire compassion.

In Buddhism, birth and death are seen as illusory. Our True Nature or Buddha Nature is untouched and goes beyond birth and death. Realisation, referred to as awakening or enlightenment, is similar to waking up and realising that we have taken our dreams to be real. We continue in this cycle of birth and death over many lifetimes until we are able to realise our True Nature. This is referred to as samsara, a Sanskrit word describing the repetitive cycle of birth, death and rebirth arising from our attachments to this world. It is the realm of **relative truth** and the illusory world. Buddha found a way to step out of the confusion of samsara into the light and freedom of Nirvana, the realm of **absolute truth**, through non-attachment, wisdom and compassion. This is called Dharma, the teachings of the Buddha. It involves taming and training our hearts and minds in order to penetrate to a deeper level of understanding of life and death. As described earlier, this is through following the Buddhist path, and by developing compassion and awareness, through reflection and meditation. However, to follow Dharma to its ultimate goal, Nirvana, beyond the reach of death, involves a long and often challenging journey of working with and transforming our accumulated habits of thinking and behaving – the aspects that obscure us and keep us trapped within samsara.

In Buddhism, awakening to our True Nature is reached through the path of Dharma with the support of the Sangha – a community who also follow the path of awakening and provide us with a living connection to it.

Reflective exercise

Just pause a moment and spend a moment settling yourself in a way that works for you. You may want to focus on your breath. As you do this, see if you can connect with that deeper part of yourself that knows – your True Nature – just sense into this and see what arises. See if you can sense into this in your body. Rest in this for a few minutes. As you do that, notice any images, feelings, sensations, however fleeting, that may arise. You may want to make some notes for yourself. There is no right or wrong way. It's what works for you.

Crossing the river: death and dying

In the last section we looked at the importance of compassion and awakening to our True Nature within the Buddhist path of spirituality. The nature and process of death and dying are central to Buddhism. This section gives a brief overview of death and dying as part of the Buddhist path, and the importance of compassion in that process.

Death is the last experience of this life. From a Buddhist perspective there is no reason to think that our consciousness does not continue after death. The fundamental nature of awareness, the basis of all our experience, does not change at death, any more than it changes from moment to moment in this life, and from thought to thought. The only difference is what appears within it. This is known through practising meditation and reflecting on our experience, by which we come to understand the fundamental nature of awareness, our True Nature, whose essence is compassion. When we realise our True Nature is fundamental and unchanging, we can realise how birth and death are illusory – appearances within awareness, like images in a mirror. This realisation enables us to cross the river from life to death with more compassion, more seamlessly, and with more ease. This truth can be glimpsed even in this life and can be enough to give us confidence in the path to awakening. That confidence can then also carry us across the river, through both life and death.

Buddhism could be said to be about death and the path that leads beyond it. In a sense, we are experiencing a kind of death from moment to moment as we let go of our thought world to meditation and when we sleep. However, our fundamental awareness arising from our True Nature is always there – we are just not necessarily consciously connected to it. As mentioned earlier, it is a bit like the clouds and the sun; the sun is always shining, but can be, and often is, obscured by clouds. So it is with our True Nature. From a Buddhist perspective death is not the end, merely a change of consciousness from one life to another. As we take on a new incarnation or rebirth, that fundamental awareness does not go anywhere – it remains.

The Buddhist teachings on the stages of the process of dying and beyond are described as the 'Bardos'. While there is a basic death process that happens to every human being, the exact sequence, timings and how it is actually experienced can vary enormously from person to person. The Bardo states are listed in the appendices.

The important message here is that from a Buddhist perspective, awareness, our fundamental and True Nature, is unchanged by death. It is this we need to trust as we face death.

The Buddhist perspective on death and dying emphasises:

- The importance of impermanence and the illusory nature of this life. This encourages us to let go of attachment to this life, and helps us open up to the path of awakening, and through meditation, to learn to rest in our compassionate hearts.

■ At death, everyone experiences what is called 'Clear Light', but for many it is a fleeting experience that goes unnoticed. When it shines through vividly, it is called 'Clear Light Mind'. It is also called the 'Indestructible Heart Essence' to emphasise its unchanging essence, and that it is found at the very core of our being, otherwise known as our Buddha Nature. Because all things emerge from it, it is also called the 'Primordial Ground'.

■ Our True Nature, the very essence of our being is often referred to in Buddhism as the 'awakened heart'. There are many terms for this. Our essence is therefore love and compassion, which never dies. These are timeless qualities emanating from a person's True Nature. However, we need to trust our compassionate heart, rely on our heart connections and our True Nature and let go when we go through the process of death. It is in trusting our heart, our True Nature, our inner wisdom, love, compassion and heart connections that our eternal nature is revealed. We facilitate our trust in and connection to our True Nature through applying meditation and compassion practices.

Spirituality, Buddhism and psychological therapies

In the last sections we looked at some key cornerstones of Buddhism, including death and dying and the importance of compassion within the Buddhist path of spirituality. This final section looks at spirituality and how aspects of Buddhism, compassion in particular, are being adapted and incorporated into some mainstream areas. The example here is within psychological therapies.

Over the last 15 years aspects of Eastern traditions, and in particular Buddhism, have been incorporated into key psychological therapies, such as compassion, (compassion-focused therapy, (Gilbert, (2010)) mindfulness, (mindfulness-based stress reduction, Kabat-Zinn (1990); dialectical behaviour therapy, (Linehan, (1999)), and acceptance (acceptance and commitment therapy, (Hayes *et al*, 1999)). There is a growing evidence base for their effectiveness in helping a person work with and manage their distress.

Spirituality and psychological therapies are therefore a developing area and has been addressed more fully elsewhere (Gilbert, 2011, Chapter 9)

The salient emerging spiritual psychology is compassion (Gilbert, 2009). Compassionate practices, as discussed earlier, are central to most Buddhist traditions. Peter strove to embody both compassion and acceptance with all the people he worked with, and particularly his work in mental health within the NHS.

Paul Gilbert (2009) has developed compassion-focused therapy (Gilbert, 2010), a psychological therapy which has developed an evidence base, demonstrating positive changes in the brain and neural pathways as a result of engaging in compassion-focused therapy (CFT). CFT helps us understand the nature of our distress and suffering based on an evolutionary model of three emotional regulation systems. It helps us to see that compassion and compassionate skills are ones we can learn and practise by deliberately and consciously making compassionate choices to cope with and transform our distress and suffering. We can learn to pay compassionate attention, to think compassionately, to engage in compassionate behaviour and practise compassionate feeling. In developing compassionate feeling we can practise compassionate imagery and sensory focusing. The capacity to learn these skills arises from our inherently compassionate nature and heart, that part of ourselves with which we have lost connection.

There is growing evidence that compassion-focused therapy helps a range of people who are experiencing depression, anxiety, and other problems such as psychosis, to improve their well-being (Gilbert, 2010).

Reflective exercise

Spend a few moments settling yourself and let your attention rest in your heart. Allow yourself space to connect with your compassionate self. Spend a few moments sensing, embracing and breathing in those qualities. They may be qualities such as warmth, care, kindness and tenderness. If you have difficulty with this, think about someone who for you represents compassion. This may be someone you know or a famous figure such as Nelson Mandela or the Dalai Lama. Get a sense of their qualities and allow these to touch your heart. If it helps, make some notes.

Concluding reflections

This chapter began by outlining some key aspects of Buddhism in relation to the themes covered in this chapter. Within spirituality and in particular the Tibetan Buddhist tradition, our True Nature, whose essence is compassion and never dies – it is eternal, as is expressed by the extract from the poem, *The Prophet* (Gibran, 1926).

On death

'You would know the secret of death.
But how shall you find it unless you seek it in the heart of life?
The owl whose night-bound eyes are blind unto the day cannot unveil the mystery
of light.
If you would indeed behold the spirit of death, open your heart wide unto the body
of life.
For life and death are one, even as the river and sea are one.'
(Kahil Gibran, *The Prophet*)

It is through trusting, cultivating and nurturing our compassionate heart on the path to awakening that we transform our suffering and connect with our True Nature, in both life and death.

In this chapter we have also briefly looked at how aspects of Buddhism and particularly compassion are being applied in areas such as psychological therapies to help people with their suffering. The mental health field and mental health services generally are beginning to recognise the crucial part compassion has to play in working with and helping those who are suffering. This is reflected, for example, in government recommendations following the Francis Report (2013), outlining the gross mistreatment of patients at Mid Staffordshire Hospital. There has been an acknowledgement that staff and organisations need to be working more compassionately.

In today's fast-changing, and turbulent world, there is a growing call and need for us as individuals, for businesses, healthcare – in fact all organisations – to awaken to our True Nature and meaningfully embody some of the principles of Buddhism, such as compassion. In that way we will begin collectively to reduce and transform our suffering and increase our well-being.

Appendices

1. Compassion, teachings and practices: These are within the Tibetan Buddhist tradition and are developed through Lojong (training the mind). The main teachings in this are:

■ The seven points of mind training

■ The eight verses

■ Turning suffering and happiness into enlightenment

   The main practices are loving-kindness and tonglen.

2. The four phases of the Bardos:

   1. The dissolution process, which comprises the inner and outer dissolutions
   2. The actual moment of death
   3. The intermediate state after death
   4. Rebirth

   (Hookham, 2006)

References

Francis R (2013) *Report of the Mid Staffordshire NHS Foundation Trust Public Inquiry*. London: Crown Copyright.

Gibran K (1926) *The Prophet*. London: Heinemann.

Gilbert P (2011) *Spirituality and Mental Health*. Brighton: Pavillion.

Gilbert P (2010) *Compassion Focused Therapy: The CBT distinctive series*. London: Routledge.

Gilbert P (2009) *The Compassionate Mind*. London: Constable.

Hayes S, Strosahl KD & Wilson KG (1999) *Acceptance and Commitment Therapy*. London: Routledge.

Hookham, LS (2006) *There's More to Dying than Death*. Birmingham: Windhorse publications. (See Chapter 3 for more detail on death and dying.)

Kabat-Zinn J (1990) *Full Catastrophe Living: How to cope with stress, pain and illness using mindfulness meditation*. London: Paitkus.

Linehan MM (1999) *Dialectic Behaviour Therapy*. London: Guildford Press.

Neff K (2011) *Self Compassion: A healthier way of relating to yourself*. USA: William Morrow.

Rinpoche S (1992) *The Tibetan Book of Living and Dying*. London: Rider. (See Chapter 12 for compassion practices.)

Rinpoche TT (2007) *Compassion Conquers All: Teachings on the eight verses of mind training*. Selangor: Kechara.

Further resources

The Francis Report: www.midstaffspublicinquiry.com/

Kongtrul J (1987) *The Great Path of Awakening*. Massachusetts USA: Shambhala. (Teachings on the Seven Points of Mind Training.)

Rinpoche YM (2007) *The Joy of Living*. New York: Harmony.

Spirituality and leadership

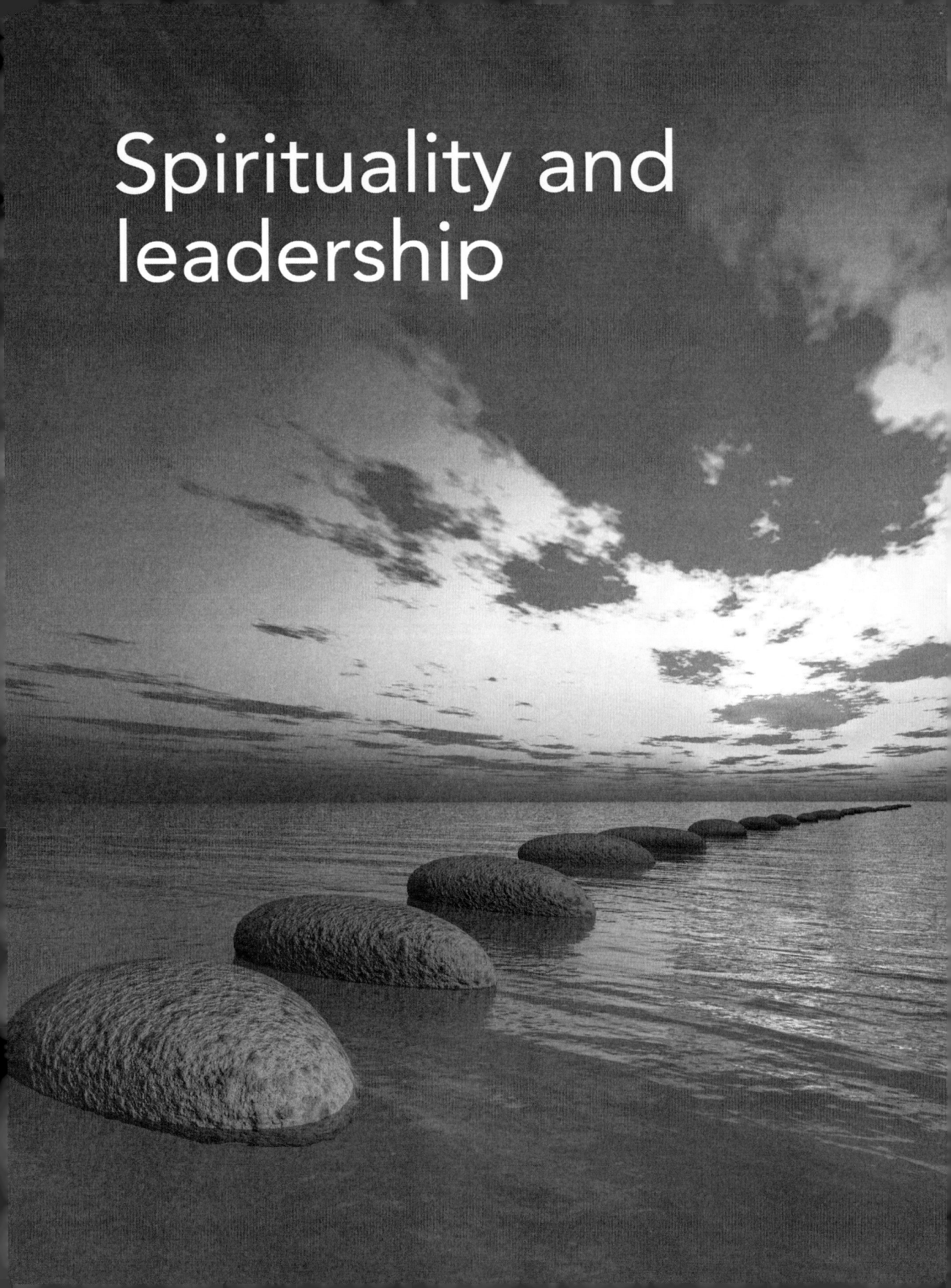

Chapter 13: The river's flow: life and leadership personified

Bhai Sahib Dr Mohinder Singh

Waters of humility

Water is the lifeblood of creation; without it all would be inanimate and barren. Despite the simple chemical formula of H_2O, we cannot create it in its miraculous abundance. Flowing water reflects many precious qualities in the human being. In Sikh teaching, its free and continuous movement downwards is analogous to humility. Humility awakens a deep recognition of one's place within the vast context of humanity and the infinite context of existence. A person characterised by humility naturally seeks to be of service to others, remains ever 'in flow' without stagnating. Such a person has the calming, cooling and restorative effect of a refreshing stream. Like life-giving water, humility sustains and keeps buoyant a human being's core spiritual attributes. According to Sikh *dharam* or faith, it is the practice of these attributes which enables us to 'live in God's image' and fulfil our purpose as sparks of the divine, blessed with the gift and responsibility of human life.

As I picture Peter Gilbert now, the portrait I see is painted by these very 'waters of humility'. I met with Peter on a number of occasions through his work with the National Spiritual and Mental Health Forum and his writings on leadership. I was struck by his genuine kind-heartedness and gift of being an extremely attentive listener. His warm and open nature meant that people were easily drawn to him. He went beyond dogma and doctrine to engage hands-on with practicalities. He was a doer and a leader with a human touch. His person-centred approach meant he could find alternative ways of working with people, without pigeonholing them. He also recognised and valued the faith perspective, and did not pigeonhole that either. Even when he could not be recompensed for his work, he continued to serve with passion, perseverance and sheer tenacity of will.

A shared wavelength, concurrent themes

Such qualities were the engine behind Peter's dynamic, socially transformative work and also made way for the great synergy we experienced in our meetings. Peter had been intrigued by the approaches of our Sikh faith-led organisation to enhance social provisioning for the common good, by innovating through concepts and practices drawn from our spiritual heritage. In Handsworth, Birmingham, this has taken the form of five centres for excellence, where the spiritual hub of the gurudwara has supported the emergence of the Nishkam centre for civic and interfaith engagement, a self-help community co-operative for employment, and centres for health and well-being, for education and, a project still in progress, care for the elderly (see Gilbert, 2009). Peter came to be a real friend and supporter and, since coming to know us, somehow kept us in his loop and on his radar. The driving ethos for our work is *nishkam sewa*, or serving others actively and altruistically. Selflessly motivated action, which transcends limitations and thrives through sparking meaningful connections, is something Peter so naturally personified, turning a theoretical principle into a workable, social legacy.

Water travels also as waves and it was the sense of shared wavelength with Peter that seemed to illuminate and energise our parallel endeavours. The scope of Peter's concurrent interests, from mental health to social health, guided by spiritually aware and spiritually nourished leadership, struck many chords with us. His recognition of such resonance revealed his ability to get under the skin of cultural or professional differences and be a catalyst for collaboration and change. This chapter courses a small journey through some of the themes in Peter's work that were of mutual interest, and mutually valued as vital for a healthy and flourishing self and society.

Public and community leadership

Peter's examination of faith-inspired leadership (Gilbert, 2009) was a bold testament to his conviction that spirituality and secularity do and should mix for the common good. He rationalised this in simple and accessible terms in the preamble to the text of the interview conducted with me. Outlining the loss of reality, of meaning, of community and of trust which characterises contemporary leadership challenges, he pointed to the need for leadership with authenticity and integrity, and with a human face. He encouraged readers to see the value of faith-inspired leadership, both in terms of the overarching and integrated view it takes of human existence and human thriving, and in terms of the strengths that can be drawn from faith-inspired communities.

In the course of the interview I discussed what I saw as the ingredients of good leadership. From a faith-perspective, it consists of seeing one's role as a genuine duty and responsibility, with love and compassion as the driving force. It requires humility with zero arrogance, the ability to listen, obey and serve others, before starting to direct others, and leading with passion, rather than through a remote control, armchair strategy. In the context of the Sikh faith, leadership of one's own faith community must entail working to further the well-being of all communities (*sarbat da bhalla*), hence our local efforts are undertaken with the aim of providing an anchor of regeneration for the wider local community. The honour of receiving a Queen's Award for Voluntary Service (2010) helps to demonstrate, we feel, the unique strengths of being positioned in the third sector, alongside the private and public sectors with their respective strengths and shortfalls.

The idea of leadership undertaken in a spirit of service to others is brought out in Peter's in-depth study of leadership (Gilbert, 2005): *'Leadership is never something that you grasp for yourself, but is a privilege and a gift, ultimately conferred on us by those we serve'*. I would add that it requires a 'trialogue' beyond human-to-human interaction, which includes a relationship with God, or one's sense of a divine transcendent. This spurs us to steadfastly strive to embody what is good and right by keeping our values-base firmly in sight. From the Sikh viewpoint, this arises from a sense of gratitude, responsibility and accountability to a higher power, whose latent presence within us is kindled through the practice of virtue. Peter's leadership was dedicated to the identification and spread of good practice, by connecting the centre with frontline work in the regions. His work certainly gave voice and recognition to our aspirations as a community-based organisation, small enough to be close to the grassroots and significant enough to make a difference through partnerships with larger scale guiding institutions.

Leadership of the self

Peter rightly pointed out the need to lead oneself before one leads others. This is a key theme in Sikh teaching, expressed in our way of life by, for example, the wearing of the *dastar* or turban. In eastern cultures especially it has long marked the qualities of sovereignty, wisdom, responsibility and accomplishment. The turban is worn by Sikhs irrespective of social status, with the idea that everybody deserves dignity and to earn respect through practising noble virtues. Leadership of the self requires the skills of the 'saint-soldier' to overcome internally the reverse pull of the negative ego, or the I-am-ness which we call *haumai*. Part and parcel of our being, *haumai*, is a force which must come under our wise and judicious control, rather than overpowering us and driving our thoughts and actions.

Just as good leaders unleash the best in the communities they serve, so we as individuals must curtail the negative and magnify the positive inside us. This is not an isolated effort; it requires social environments conducive to bringing the best out in us. In a powerful way, Peter triggered changes in the culture of doing things, bringing more selflessness and empathy to the fore. He encouraged people at all levels to see the bigger picture of one's values-base and one's interdependent existence alongside others. He echoed my sentiment that leadership requires nurture, through practical education and lifelong exposure and that to find effective leaders is not a 'shelf-picking' exercise. Thus he demonstrated the Sikh principle that the best education for leadership is learnt through our lived association, or what we term as *sangat*, with other humans, beyond the textbook or tick box exercise approach.

Mental and holistic well-being

The implications of Peter's work, connecting spirituality with mental health, are far-reaching. He transcended excessively bureaucratic and clinical interpretations of health conditions, and opened up new pathways for solutions. He exemplified ways to harness the less tangible human and social dimension to restore a sense of wholeness and well-being by attending to the welfare of the spirit. This has been echoed in our own Nishkam initiatives to bring to the fore the less recognised power of lived values. We have set in motion a series of projects to nurture the very young, engage with and care for the elderly, and provide opportunities for people of all ages to experience the fulfilment that comes from meaningful work and contributing to the lives of others. The role of faith communities in addressing social challenges has been recognised in a recent report by the leading cross-party think-tank, Demos (Birdwell with Timms, 2013), as well as Peter's own contribution to essays on the role of faith in society (Gilbert, 2013a).

The mind, as the driver of our thoughts, actions and deeds, is intertwined with the life of our spirit. Its ability to make choices, to adopt habits, to 'hold the reins' of how we think, feel and act in response to the world around us, can allow us to either neglect, or to nourish the spirit. Yet, conversely, a well-nourished spirit helps to transform the mind, by changing the conditions of our internal environment. In the mind-related vocabulary of the Punjabi language, we talk of *surti-birti*; *surti* suggests the focus of one's mind and *birti*, the overall ethos or condition of the mind in terms of the values and experiences that steer it. Peter made way for doing things differently in our social settings and systems, by adjusting our lenses and bringing change to the ethos of our mental and social environment. He was able to indicate how the mind and spirit work in tandem and to chalk out approaches to recognise and optimise this partnership. This follows a faith-inspired conviction I have long held, that social cohesion depends on finding cohesion within ourselves, when we recognise and build on the interdependence of our body, spirit and mind.

Peter himself had described his experience of depression as the result of a 'disconnection' at many levels. In the Guru Granth Sahib (the sacred text we Sikhs revere as Guru), the journey of our inward and outward existence is likened to a tumultuous and treacherous ocean, where faith provides direction and insights, motivation and companionship, along with hope and trust, to keep one afloat and carry one across. It can expand and strengthen a positive sense of self by renewing a sense of connectivity with the self, the world and the sacredness which supports and transcends it. Peter's ability to describe how a faith-rich environment facilitated his recovery provided a personal starting point to acknowledge the valuable role of faith in restoring a sense of wholeness. It was also a reminder that we all stand to some degree on a knife's edge of being mentally stable or unstable, and need strategies and spaces embedded in our everyday lives that keep us and save us from sinking.

Widening the currency of faith-inspired concepts

As a Sikh faith-led organisation we have sought to highlight the integral importance of spirituality to everyday secular and social life. Peter's articulations have helped to create a public pathway for such viewpoints to be meaningfully listened to and taken on board. I would echo the words of Neil Deuchar in his epilogue to *Spirituality and End of Life Care* (Gilbert, 2013b), that Peter created *'a construct and a vocabulary'* to discuss issues about spiritual and religious life, which might otherwise be dismissed at their slightest mention, and that through his personal and professional contributions, he has been able to accelerate the pace of change. This is heartening for us as a faith rooted in a lesser known language and culture. Peter was readily able to see the broader social relevance of the ethos and values underpinning our distinctively expressed faith.

The river and the ocean

As every one of us comes to face eternity and the finite nature of our physical existence, the role of continuity is given to our spirit. The spirit sums up for others the essence of the person we have been and have become in this life, and the kind of legacy we will leave for others. From the Sikh faith perspective, the flourishing of the spirit arises from the exercising of our innate spiritual attributes. These constitute the only wealth that accompanies us at the end of our sojourn here on the planet. Emanating, as we as Sikhs understand it, from God, our lived virtues reconnect us with our Creator, just as rays of light connect up with the sun, and rivers flow back into the ocean. Peter's expansiveness and compassionate influence flows over and beyond a single life. In this way he epitomises a picture of life's fulfilment, according to Sikh teaching, where the amazing opportunity of human existence is made worthy and whole through the difference one is blessed to make to others.

References

Birdwell J with Timms S (2013) *The Faith Collection: Exploring the role of faith in British society and politics*. London: DEMOS.

Gilbert P (2005) *Leadership: Being effective and remaining human*. Dorset: Russell House Publishing.

Gilbert P (2009) Interview: Bhai Sahib Dr Mohinder Singh'. *International Journal of Leadership in Public Services* **5** (2) 38–42.

Gilbert P (2013a) Attending to the spirit in mental health. In D Singleton (Ed) *Faith with its Sleeves Rolled Up*. London: Faith Action Books.

Gilbert P (ed) (2013b) *Spirituality and End of Life Care*. Brighton: Pavilion Publishing.

Chapter 14: Cynicism, leadership and integrity

Peter Sedgwick

Peter Gilbert: A resource for an organisation in rapid change

Peter Gilbert gave some very helpful talks at St. Michael's College, Cardiff, in 2005 on leadership, which grew out of his work in local authorities. I turned to Peter because in my previous role as policy officer for mental health in the Church of England over nearly a decade, there had been a trio of Arthur Hawes, Peter and myself, which had achieved a great deal. The college in 2005 was beginning the process of change from being entirely a residential college which trained people for the Anglican priesthood (and prior to 1995 those people were only men) to being a theological institute which worked with people of all faiths, provided higher degrees in partnership with Cardiff University, was a welcoming and professional conference centre, and still retained its original function of training men and women for ordained ministry. In 2005 we were at the beginning of a great deal of change, which in the last decade has seen our turnover nearly treble, and the college change out of all recognition. We needed someone like Peter to begin this process, and Peter was inspirational in helping us see what was needed.

In essence we wanted to change, while keeping true to what we had been and the values which underpinned this. The question was whether that was possible? Would we simply become another higher education institution, losing touch with the church we had served for a century and the values that had been embodied in this? Were there also values in that church which themselves were in need of renewal, and which fed clericalism, dependence and passivity? What was needed was a lengthy process of bringing about change, while writing a vision and values statement that could guard our own integrity. Peter began this process, and the input from him at the very beginning was very helpful.

Cynicism in the modern organisation

This article considers how integrity, both individually and corporately, is one of the great issues in contemporary organisations. People's cynicism is sadly often all too justified, in terms of the way in which many leaders do lead without any obvious values. One can think of many politicians, whose personal and public failings only make them all the more visible in the public eye, as Damian McBride has recently graphically demonstrated in terms of what he calls *'the personal feuds, political plots, and media manipulation which lay at New Labour's core'* (McBride, 2013). Such lack of values can be found in many political parties and businesses. They can also sadly be found in religious bodies, as the cover up of child abuse graphically demonstrates, and even in charities. Yet cynicism is destructive on every front, not only in terms of religious and caring organisations, but also in terms of how any organisation (political, business or corporate) can justify its own existence to its employees and those whom it serves.

In the secular world of corporate leadership, there is much on lack of integrity. Donna Markham (1999, p120–121) describes the leader who has deep-seated feelings about being inauthentic and inadequate. The substance of personal identity and inner authority is lacking. They become successful by becoming nurturing and consultative, but the very process of consultation leads to a drawing back from the process of transformational change. Nevertheless, while Markham is acute in her observation, and the need to be able to handle conflict, what is striking is the absence of a strong value base in her account of leadership. Equally, the powerful and much used book *The Five Dysfunctions of a Team* (Lencioni, 2002) has a great deal on absence of trust; fear of conflict; lack of commitment; avoidance of accountability; and finally inattention to results. What there is not is any in-depth discussion of personal values and integrity. Commitment is lacking in a team because people have not *'unloaded their opinions and feel they've been listened to'* (Lencioni, 2002, p94). What matters is not what one agrees on, but whether, after an intense discussion, there is commitment. This may be an effective strategy for bringing people on board in terms of leadership, but it leads to ignoring the principles which should inform any organisation. This is especially the case when, as Peter points out, there are high levels of employee cynicism at work. Corporate pronouncements around values, ethics, diversity policies and inclusion are greeted with scepticism (Gilbert, 2005, p30).

This is even more acute as there are changing values in society, a lack of trust in the leaders of society, and a general anxiety about what is perceived as *'an ethic of aggression'*. Organisations spend greater amounts of effort seeking to persuade their workforce to accept more change, but the result is that relationships are seen as transactional and disconnected. While it is true that absence of trust can, and does, spring from a culture of not making oneself vulnerable, the danger of demonstrating personal and corporate vulnerability without any commitment to integrity and values can be self-defeating. One searches in vain for a discussion of values and integrity in Lencioni's book. This absence of integrity is especially highlighted by a study of the many scandals and fraud in American business in the last two decades (Byron, 2006).

Byron describes in great detail the scandals of Enron, World Com, and many others. What is so striking is that the lamentable failings of modern business were exposed by this experienced academic (a Jesuit who became a professor of business ethics in many business schools in the US) in his book in 2006, two years before the great banking crash which dragged the whole world into financial catastrophe. In spite of his warning, and those of many others, the whole financial system in 2008 fell over a cliff, driven by greed and cynicism. Byron is clear that it is lack of integrity which has damaged modern organisations. He writes as a long-standing faculty member of an American business school. Byron argues that the greatest need is to regain a sense of integrity in modern corporations.

Byron looks at how Enron corrupted the accounting firm Arthur Andersen, which was meant to preserve the financial probity and veracity of Enron. Its collusion in wrongdoing led *to its honesty, integrity and general competence* to be called into question (Byron, 2006, p33). Byron shows that there are two aspects of integrity. One is corporate, and the other is personal. Both demand consistency between values and actions, over time. Such consistency brings stability and predictability to the organisation being led, so that even in the midst of rapid change, there are moral compasses against which decisions are made. (Byron, 2006, p35). This leads into a reflection on honesty. Byron quotes the Woodstock Theological Center: *'Honesty requires the avoidance of deception and careless misrepresentation of information on which others may rely. Communications, both internal and external, should be truthful and accurate … In some cases; honesty may require specific disclosures, so that affected parties will have access to relevant information'* (Byron, 2006, p40).

Peter spoke at a conference in 2012 sponsored by Transformational Leadership in Care entitled 'Leading with Integrity in Uncertain Times'. The conference argued that: *'Integrity is an essential ingredient of leadership. It inspires trust, confidence and respect and brings out the very best in others. Lack of integrity inevitably leads to manipulation, cynicism and demoralisation. The issue is how do we manage services in a way which does not compromise or undermine the values which lie at the heart of social work? How do we sustain ourselves and lead from a position of inner strength, clarity and confidence?'* The danger is that the management of change becomes coercive, and imposes itself.

Here, cynicism is not caused by the outright manipulation and dishonesty of politicians, as McBride describes above in reference to the Labour Government of 2000–2010. Rather it is created by the persistent compromises in the delivery of care services, which in an era of cuts and lack of resources means that the leader is seen to have a lack of integrity. In turn, this develops into a growth of cynicism, both within the organisation and by those who depend on it. The issue of preserving integrity in a contemporary culture that lacks a clear ethical rationale remains absolutely central in leadership. In summary, to quote another talk given by Peter in May 2013: *'Leadership with integrity means that leaders are self-aware, have a clear value-base and work towards a defined vision and empowering service. Leaders "walk-the-talk", and live the values they espouse. The opposite of leadership with integrity is what he called inauthentic leadership. The vision statement becomes meaningless, and diverse voices are crushed'* (Gilbert, 2013). The result inevitably is the growth of cynicism.

Integrity and spirituality

The talks given by Peter to St. Michael's College and to other organisations were written up in his wonderful book, *Leadership: Being effective and remaining human* (Gilbert, 2005). He stressed four aspects of leadership: personal and professional integrity; values, especially as they are demonstrated in the workplace; ethical decision making; and the importance of self-awareness. Peter did not see this as different from spirituality. These aspects of leadership were a lived and embodied spirituality. The issue of building and preserving integrity therefore always leads into the question of spirituality. Spirituality can be seen in purely secular terms as the living out of what those inside and outside the organisation can see as embodied integrity. It can also be rephrased (in religious language) so that uniting integrity and spirituality focuses on the service of one's neighbour. This can be put both in secular language, but also in theological language, because as this chapter shows, Peter crossed this boundary with ease again and again. Theology and secular language were one world for him, and he fused them together in a unique and deeply compelling way. In secular terms, it is at least in the words of one leadership theory *'the singer, not the song'* (Gilbert, 2005, p43). If one had to justify the juxtaposition of the deeply religious and the very secular, it is shown in the way Peter's book compares Cardinal Basil Hume and the 2004 English rugby team (Gilbert, 2005, p50).

Peter's argument was that the word 'leadership' is derived from the old English word 'laedan': a road, a way, the path of a ship at sea, and is related to another old English word 'lithan' – 'to travel'. So, a leader is a person who discovers the right direction in which to travel (integrity); takes other people with them; guides them and supports them on the journey; and keeps the goal always in the mind's eye (the vision) (Gilbert, 2005, p4). Quoting Chris Lake of Roffey Park Management Institute, he argued that leaders were people with high self-esteem, whose actions are congruent with their espoused views, who understand their own beliefs and values and who have a strong sense of their own direction. To be truly effective as a leader, you've got to be comfortable with who you are and what you are about. Essentially, concentrating on leading yourself is a powerful way to grow your ability to lead others. What is striking about Peter's argument is how value-driven he was.

Personal integrity was something which, he argued, stemmed from inhabiting, and being comfortable within a positive value base, which in turn was embodied in personal self-modelling. One of the most striking things about Peter was his ability to live both in the secular world of social services, and organisational culture, and yet keep a deep-rootedness in the Catholic monastic tradition. This was especially shown in his many links with Worth Abbey. A recent study of monastic spirituality explored the reason why monasticism has retained its appeal and it echoed much of what Peter found there. Grimley writes: *'There has been an explosion of interest in the benefits and fruits of monastic spirituality and culture, both in its historical and contemporary contexts. Even where people have given up on the institutional churches, monasticism retains an integrity and magnetic appeal ... (It) makes monastic spirituality so attractive to so many people ... it can be incorporated into an individual's everyday life in practical ways'* (Grimley & Wooding, 2010).

What did Peter mean when he wrote about spirituality? He wrote often about the term. Spirituality is for him the awareness of an inner spirit and value, which was the motivating force and ultimate meaning of our lives, thus shaping all that we do. Such an appeal to a life-force is not an appeal to a mere source of energy, or vitalism. It was fully imbued with value, and so with ethical integrity (Gilbert, 2011, p24). He could find spirituality in the major philosophical traditions of the West, but also in the world religions, citing the Qur'an, where Allah breathes 'ruh' into each human being. He especially drew on the definition of the Royal College of Psychiatrists, which says: *'Spirituality is a distinctive, potentially creative and universal dimension of human experience arising both within the inner subjective awareness of individuals and within communities, social groups and traditions'* (Gilbert, 2011, p30).

The Christian tradition: a footnote

In around the year 200CE Clement of Alexandria wrote a guide for those who had become Christians, and who were themselves persons of wealth and high social standing. It was called *The Instructor*, or *Pedagogos*. Many of those for whom it was written exercised leadership, either social or political. Clement was aware that spirituality will lack integrity if it becomes compatible with almost any form of life. Clement's targets are in one way obvious, such as luxury and the love of riches, manipulation and dishonesty. We are back to the 'power trip' so graphically portrayed by McBride (2013). Little has changed in 2,000 years. However there is nothing in Clement's account about how leadership might be exercised in organisations.

Things change dramatically by the sixth century Rule of St. Benedict, much quoted by Peter in his writings on leadership, and also a great personal resource for him from his association with the Benedictine Worth Abbey. Benedict is insistent on two things. First, the practices of Benedict's Rule are not ways of dealing with luxury and the indulgences offered by power (though that might not be a bad thing in the hedonism of Western cultural life today) nor are they practices that elevate one in virtue. They are there so that practices can change our beliefs, and find Christ in new and unexpected places – in the most menial of the workforce, in the most difficult of clients, in the service of others. Second, they are there so that a lifetime of repeated and disciplined practices lead to an unself-conscious practice of humility, integrity and listening to others (Coakley, 2002). As she writes on the integration of spirituality, integrity and practice: *'The logical relation of practices to beliefs becomes one of mutual interaction. More or less subliminally and with a loosening of previous moral judging, the inner meanings of belief start to make their impact: Christ ceases to be merely an external model to be imitated, but is recognised in the poor, the stranger at the gate'* (Coakley, 2002, p86).

If Coakley is right, the answer to cynicism is the daily practice and endless repetition of leadership, integrity and spirituality as a single whole. So the theological expression of this would be the daily taking up of the cross in complete integrity as the self-redeemed by Christ encounters whatever the workplace throws at him, or her. It becomes the pursuit of 'active holiness'. Peter drew deeply on this Christian tradition (Gilbert, 2005, p51; Gilbert & Jolly, 2004). It is worth ending with a quote from the book written by Peter and Dom Luke Jolly OSB on the relevance of the Rule in the modern organisation: *'Leadership, with its accent on values, direction, inspiration and delivery, is essential in a world where change is constant, public expectations are high, and people to deliver a service are in short supply'* (Gilbert & Jolly, 2004). That is the answer to organisational cynicism; that style of leadership embodies integrity; that integrity is lived spirituality. The article comes together, quite appropriately, in one man: Peter Gilbert.

References

Byron W (2006) *The Power of Principles: Ethics for the new corporate culture*. New York: Orbis Books.

Coakley S (2002) Deepening practices: perspectives from ascetical and mystical theology. In: M Volf and D Bass (eds) *Practicing Theology: Beliefs and practices in the Christian life*. Grand Rapids, MI: Eerdmans.

Gilbert P & Jolly DL (2004) *Serving to Lead: St. Benedict and servant leadership*. Worth Abbey Publications.

Gilbert P (2005) *Leadership: Being effective and remaining human*. London: Russell House Publishing.

Gilbert P (2011) Understanding mental health and spirituality. In: Peter Gilbert (ed) *Spirituality and Mental Health*. Brighton: Pavilion Publishing.

Gilbert P (2013) *Treat Me as You Would Wish to be Treated*. Worcestershire Health Watch Launch, 10 May 2013. Available at: http://www.healthwatchworcestershire.co.uk/sites/default/files/professor_peter_gilbert_presentation_0.pdf (accessed December 2013).

Grimley A & Wooding J (2010) *Living the Hours: Monastic spirituality in everyday life*. Norwich: The Canterbury Press.

Lencioni P (2002) *The Five Dysfunctions of a Team*. San Francisco: Jossey-Bass.

Markham DJ (1999) *Spirit-linking Leadership*. Mahwah, New Jersey: Paulist Press.

McBride D (2013) *Power Trip: A decade of policy, plots and spin*. London: Biteback Press.

Woodstock Theological Center (1990) *Creating and Maintaining an Ethical Corporate Culture*. Washington, DC: Georgetown University Press.

Chapter 15: Leadership in learning disability services

Peter Bates

Introduction

Peter Gilbert became an associate at the National Development Team for Inclusion (NDTi) in 2003 and then served in the roles of chair of the board and treasurer between 2008 and 2010. The NDTi is a not-for-profit organisation concerned with promoting inclusion and equality for people who risk exclusion and who need support to lead a full life. We have a particular interest in issues around age, disability, mental health, and children and young people. Throughout his time with NDTi, Peter persistently encouraged us to think about leadership.

Distributed leadership we can all share

The last decade has seen a dramatic reframing of the concept of leadership in the political context as well as in social care, moving from remote senior managers who exercise control by issuing commands to situational, nearby, emergent and distributed leadership that is recognised by others rather than asserted by the leader themselves (Alban-Metcalfe & Alimo-Metcalfe, 2009). This kind of leadership combines being and doing; character and skills; relationships and tasks. Rather than being claimed by the leader, it is ascribed by the led, as they recognise the personal integrity of the leader and are inspired and energised to get the thing done. Sometimes the things that get done are the best of the things that they themselves have been meaning to do, but have not hitherto undertaken, as the leader helps them distil their own aspiration into action.

Distributed leadership is demonstrated when everyone takes a turn at leading and leadership is shared rather than being vested in a few high-status individuals. Day to day negotiation ensures that everyone is clear about their responsibilities and opportunities, and any confusion over who bears responsibility is tidied up through dialogue rather than job descriptions or reporting tree diagrams.

Peter was fond of drawing parallels with his running club, where the person in charge of the club was sometimes at the front, but at other times kept company with the struggler at the back, while someone else led the pack for that particular part of the run. This all sounds very egalitarian and democratic, and indeed such an approach means that high status people need to relinquish their traditional claim to power and adopt a new position of 'on tap, not on top', as Winston Churchill put it (1965). It is, of course, more difficult to create these conditions in organisations where those occupying the senior roles have more autonomy than those at the bottom of the hierarchy and where senior posts are occupied by white males, so it is perhaps unsurprising that many people adopt the cultural stereotype that defines the designated manager as the only leader.

Indeed, it is so tempting to equate leadership with 'the boss' that this error needs to be named and dismissed at the very outset. Instead, we see leadership emerging out of the unique situation in which people meet one another, build a relationship, face life together and make sense of it; especially through creating a shared story of what is happening (Bates & Gilbert, 2008). Those with high status designations must suspend rank, leave their labels 'at the door' and seek out leadership potential amongst the people with whom they interact. That leadership potential is often found in unexpected places where it can be fragile and easily squashed. Instead of presenting a paper, referencing policy, outlining commissioning intentions and showing research evidence; unlikely leaders may introduce us to their life, show us their pain and dreams, and ask us to change places with them.

So the concept of distributed leadership means that everyone – not just those on big salaries who have their own offices – can be a leader. Yes, senior managers can and must lead, but so can and must first-line managers and staff. People with learning disabilities too, can, do and must lead, along with their relatives, neighbours, work colleagues and friends.

In this chapter, we shall consider aspects of leadership by moving freely back and forth amongst these groups, from people using services to managers, from relatives to friends, from frontline staff to neighbours. Each of these groups varies from the others in the span of their leadership, as, for example, families can lead for anything up to 168 hours a week, while paid staff have less than a quarter of that available to commit to the task of leading. Each of the groups also vary in the status of their leadership. Most people expect a doctor or clinical psychologist to lead, but not many people expect a neighbour or sports buddy to exercise leadership, and so there is an additional responsibility upon people in high status roles to help create an environment where all can take their turn.

Leadership in times of austerity

The funding of social care services for people with learning disabilities is being cut. Meanwhile, the policy agenda rightly focuses upon more personalised, homely and individually designed arrangements which, as a by-product, reduce the amount of line-of-sight supervision by managers and demand new approaches to safeguarding. In addition, scandals generate repeated cycles of inspection, as if a culture of respect can be imposed from outside. In his time with the NDTi, Peter was always concerned about the quality of leadership but always matched this with an implacable demand for high quality services.

Since the Coalition Government took office in 2010, it has adopted the previous government's policy of localism and taken it further, which means that it demands outcomes but does not specify the means by which those outcomes should be achieved. It is as if we have moved from a preoccupation with processes to an utter disinterest in them, and therefore many learning disability organisations seem bewildered about how the outcomes can be achieved within the shrinking budget available. Peter would place this shift in policy in the wider panorama of history; and show how it appeared to the Greeks or perhaps the Puritans – one could never be sure which epoch he would draw from to make his point that humanity has travelled this way before. From such a historical vantage point he would notice the cyclical rhythm of these changes, alert us to anticipate the back-swing of the pendulum, and encourage us to look out for signs that both policy positions may co-exist at any one time, rather than one entirely replacing the other.

In the NDTi, we have been talking about achieving austerity with integrity. The pace of change is rapid and the unthinkable is being faced. Staff training, supervision and office buildings are disappearing. Wages are being cut. People are turned away from services. So we need to keep on listening carefully. Behind the clamour and noise of the 'ordinary' pain of recession, we still need to hear the crying out of those who suffer abuse and dangerous neglect. Peter was interested in how organisations ran, and he retained a fierce loyalty to the people using services. We share that passion.

As resources become scarcer and needs grow, we need more honesty from service leaders – people who are willing to admit exactly what is available, which needs must be met and which will not be funded from the public purse. This brutal honesty must include an accurate portrayal of the strengths and weaknesses of services. The 'gap analysis' and 'market development', so loved by commissioners, tends to be about the spread of existing service models rather than asking if they are effective. Honesty and transparency releases others to begin to think about alternative ways to address needs. So how might we answer Peter's call for leadership with humanity in support of citizens who happen to have learning disabilities? We have six steps.

1. Lead yourself

Start where Peter started – with self-leadership. In recent decades, many people with learning disabilities have acquired tenancies and mortgages; jobs and bank accounts; the right to stay up late and go home with a friend; the right to complain and instruct an advocate. Many frontline staff have embraced change by taking up different work patterns and building alliances with community groups and networks. Many families have pioneered the use of direct payments and personal health budgets and supported their disabled family member to live independently and rely less on professionals.

Take Josie's story as an example. When the learning disability hospital closed, Josie moved into her own home with support from staff who slept in the spare bedroom every night of the week. Now she and her family have embraced the next big opportunity for independence. A special touch screen on her computer allows her to phone home whenever she wants, and pressure sensors under her mattress and on the front door tell the office when she gets out of bed or leaves the house. Expensive sleepover staff are now a thing of the past and Josie has real privacy for the first time in her life. Josie's dad can't get over the joy of being phoned by his daughter, and some of the savings are being used to improve Josie's daytime opportunities.

There is no telling what courage was needed by the family to brave this journey into the unknown, when their own fears and some other parents were demanding the right to retain the old style of service and keep the sleepovers. Yet, all around the country, individuals with learning disabilities and their families are taking the lead. But much remains to be done.

2. Inquire and listen with humility

Each cut to budgets has reduced the number of managers. As their responsibility broadens, they have less time to become experts in what they do, and some appear to lack even a basic grasp of how life is lived by the people using the services that they manage. Appointment panels may select candidates for management posts who are determined to drive through cost-cutting measures rather than choosing people who can lead, listen and engage. Panels may select those candidates for frontline posts who focus on speedy task delivery rather than relationship building and respect.

Leaders need to know where to find good information and sound advice. This demands a measure of humility from leaders who are willing to admit that they do not know everything and can place themselves in a position of vulnerability by sitting with people, listening to them and asking for advice. Peter challenged people to take on new leadership responsibility while 'remaining human'. This does not sit well with the macho-aggressive culture of some service transformation teams. An aggressive culture is reinforced by:

■ confrontational political leaders who seek to differentiate between the deserving and the undeserving poor and who caricature people using services as no more than vulnerable bringers of financial ruin

■ inspection agencies that operate by inquisition and intimidation

■ tabloid journalists who seek scapegoats while engaging in lamentation and blame.

To restore a sense of hope and purpose, we need to focus on aspiration and excellence. For example, we want to know if any staff in Winterbourne View (DH, 2012) stood against the abusive culture of that organisation, and whether some teams at Mid Staffordshire Hospital (HMSO, 2013) created a counter-culture of compassion in contradistinction to the prevailing climate of neglect in the organisation at large.

So the NDTi is interested in approaches that are based on a recognition of strengths – on person-centred approaches rather than traditional care planning, on recovery rather than treatment, on asset-based community development rather than writing off 'sink neighbourhoods', and on appreciative inquiry rather than standardised audits.

It is this blend of optimism and humility that looks for leadership in unlikely places. Take, for example, the occasion when there was a need to get a message through to politicians. A traditional approach would be to lobby the high status people in society, but it turned out that people with learning disabilities could take up their own power to change the world. It happened like this.

People with learning disabilities across England were saying that dealing with hate crime was a priority for them. The senior national people in services, including those leading the Valuing People programme, were unable to even get an interview with relevant ministries like the Home Office or Ministry for Justice, to discuss action. The National Forum of People with Learning Disabilities decided to organise a campaign. They collected signatures on a petition, got press coverage, and then successfully demanded to meet with the relevant government minister. As a result, he instructed his civil servants to start taking action on the issue – self-advocates thus achieving an outcome that the national service leaders could not.

3. Find leaders in the community

Leadership needs to be found in informal communities, rather than relying too much on social care organisations. As mentioned above, Peter's much quoted running club provides the model. He looked for, and readily found, inspiration, comfort and challenge amongst the unremarkable people who made up the club, just as we all find that friendship and a shared goal add lustre to the people we treasure. We carry this forward in the inclusion work for which our organisation is named. We help staff find allies in local neighbourhoods, community organisations and faith groups so that people with learning disabilities can find real friendships in those places.

Daphne, in her 70s, started attending the local Get Together group because she felt isolated and wanted some company. This is a social gathering that is completely run by volunteers and has no fixed agenda. It quickly became apparent to the co-ordinator that Daphne was a natural leader, with an organising spirit and an inclusive and friendly approach and attitude. The co-ordinator suggested this to Daphne, who was amazed to be considered for this role as she had never been asked to lead or manage anything in her entire life, and she did not think she was 'that sort of person'. Daphne has received some training and mentoring and now not only leads a successful and expanding Get Together group, but is advising and supporting the establishment of similar gatherings across the area.

4. Build your leadership investment portfolio

Looking for leaders in new places presses us to invest in people and their ideas. Return on investment has become a popular phrase in these times of austerity, but we need to recognise that successful investment requires a blend of judgement, foresight and luck. We should judge leaders by reviewing their 'leadership investment portfolio' which identifies the people in whom they have invested their time, support and commitment – and also shows how they have learnt from their decisions over time. We need leaders who will invest in the people above them as well as below them in status or management hierarchies.

Looking for leadership in new places challenges us to adopt new approaches. We need to work together as we search for answers but also work together on uncovering the questions that should be addressed. Sometimes different groups have diverse views about what is important, as when people were asked about what was important in locked residential care units. In one review, staff on inspection teams focused on meaningful occupation, while people with learning disabilities on those teams wanted to ask residents 'Does anyone hit you?'

Experienced commentators such as John McKnight (1996) recommend that leaders need to be drawn from the local community, and staff who have no relationship with the neighbourhood or community of interest apart from their paid professional input can do little of value. This hints at a model of leadership in which people hold a diverse array of roles and interact with one another in a variety of overlapping ways (Bates, 2010) – a far cry from the professional distance that is so highly treasured in traditional services.

5. Lead for the long term

In contrast to the frantic pace of action planning and organisational restructuring, the timeframe for supporting and developing leaders is long and the pace is slow. Leaders give time to the right things, and invest in identifying, listening to and supporting community leaders who have little interest in efficient business meetings, monitoring activity via Gantt charts or writing minutes of their conversations. This process requires continuity and a time horizon that reaches well beyond the end of the current financial year or the next election. It needs leaders who will stay long enough to experience, enjoy and be accountable for their decisions. These leaders strive to demonstrate with hard evidence that their organisation's mission has been achieved and sustained over time, rather than using the role as a short-term stepping-stone to their next career move. This further emphasises the importance of nurturing people with learning disabilities and their families as leaders. They are there for the duration, with a lifelong interest in better outcomes, while paid leaders come and go.

Joan's story illustrates the value of investing in sustainable and long-term leadership. She faces a number of lifelong difficulties and so staff explained about a timebank (Cahn, 2004) where local people traded their time and talents to help one another. Joan was sceptical at first, but started talking to people about the neglected state of the nearby community garden. Her friends recognised her leadership in this project and together they tidied up the garden and planted seedlings. Both Joan and the garden have flourished and she is now an influential advocate for the timebank.

6. Leadership in my staff team and with neighbouring teams and organisations

Sharing leadership with people with learning disabilities challenges traditional power relationships. Take David's story as an example. When he applied for a job in the local psychological therapies service, he found out that he would be interviewed twice. One interview was undertaken by a panel of managers, and the second panel was formed of representatives from the local learning disability parliament. Both panels agreed that David was the best candidate for the job. After this kind of start, it is no surprise that he follows the lead of the people he serves and shapes his work according to their individual needs. For example, one person is drawing their own pictures for a personal diary as part of a behaviour activation session, while another presses David to create metaphor-free psychological treatments.

As this example reveals, the everyday decisions that once were taken by remote managers can be shared with the people who are most affected by them. This will affect not only the outcome – such as who is appointed to fill a job vacancy – but also impact people with learning disabilities, their families and the staff. It is possible to take a similar approach to decisions about training, budgets, service design and evaluation.

Not only can leadership be shared in the day-to-day operation of individual teams, but the nature of the working relationship between one team and another is affected by the idea of distributed leadership. While the UK Coalition Government has presided over some unpopular cuts in services, their policy of localism has the potential to encourage leadership via informal influence rather than command and control hierarchies. Some staff working in learning disability services report that austerity has made them less able to look beyond their own in-tray as demand increases and colleagues are made redundant. In contrast, others recognise that it was never more vital to join hands across traditional boundaries and co-ordinate efforts.

One result is that leaders who navigate between the rocks of austerity and the hard place of increasing demand are free to invent solutions that would have been unthinkable only a few years ago. It is a fertile time for new ideas, and so we need to think carefully about whether each new idea is good, or whether it might miss the underlying issue or have unintended consequences.

Take food banks as an example of this complex picture. It is terrific that Daisy, who has a learning disability, is engaged in her local church and volunteers at the local food bank where they help others feed their children. It is encouraging to see that, across the UK, communities are responding to the financial crisis by starting food banks. Indeed, the Trussell Trust report that in the last 12 months they have trebled the number of people they help and new food banks are opening at the rate of three a week. But why are they needed, what is causing so much hunger in a developed country, and what can be done to address the causes, rather than just the consequences, of poverty, unemployment and inequality? How will the food bank promote self-reliance and mutual support among its beneficiaries rather than dependence?

Conclusion

In learning disability services, the next few years will reveal whether local leaders can weave together the current opportunities that are available through personalised budgets, integration of health and social care and service withdrawal to promote meaningful lives beyond the learning disability community. It will only be possible to take such steps if local service leaders do two things. First, they must set aside their own love of control in favour of the people they support, their families and the wider community. Second, they need to share key aspects of leadership with the people and families they serve. Peter's example of life, in which he continually reflected on his core beliefs, his true motives and the effect he had on others, is surely the only way to maintain personal integrity in these challenging times.

Acknowledgements

I am indebted to Rob Greig and Bill Love from the NDTi for their help in bringing together the ideas for this chapter and to Paul Cook for his editorial support. Remaining weaknesses are, of course, my own.

References

Alban-Metcalfe J & Alimo-Metcalfe B (2009) Engaging leadership part one: competencies are like Brighton Pier. *International Journal of Leadership in Public Services* **5** (1) pp10–18.

Bates P & Gilbert P (2008) I wanna tell you a story: leaders as story-tellers *International Journal of Leadership in Public Services* **4** (2) pp4–9. DOI: 10.1108/17479886200800018.

Bates P (2010) Thinking about professional boundaries in an inclusive society. In: P Gilbert (2010) *Social Work and Mental health: The value of everything*. Lyme Regis: Russell House Publishing. Chapter 2, pp18–24.

Cahn E (2004) *No More Throw-Away People: The co-production imperative*. Washington DC: Essential Books.

Churchill, Winston, quoted in Churchill RS (1965) *Twenty-One Years* (1964). London: Weidenfeld & Nicolson, p127.

Department of Health (2012) *Transforming Care: A national response to Winterbourne View Hospital: Department of Health Review Final Report*. London: DH.

HMSO (2013) *Report of the Mid Staffordshire NHS Foundation Trust Public Inquiry: Executive summary*. Report of the Public Inquiry, chaired by Robert Francis QC. London: HMSO.

McKnight JL (1996) *The Careless Society: Community and its counterfeits*. New York: Basic Books.

Chapter 16: In my end is my beginning

Ben Bano

'In my end is my beginning.' TS Eliot, East Coker, *The Four Quartets*

A focus on our 'inner selves'

The quotation from TS Eliot which marks the title of this chapter seems particularly apt in describing Peter Gilbert's contribution to making us all aware of the importance of spirituality in every aspect of our lives.

Peter's contribution to the understanding of spirituality in the four categories discussed in this book has been clearly set in the preceding chapters. In social care practice, leadership, mental health, and interfaith relations Peter posed those 'crunch' questions which many of us may feel uncomfortable to address in an increasingly secularised world. For those in the care and other sectors who feel that organised religion has little relevance to their work, Peter broadened the question to help us to address the wider 'meaning of life' issues in an immediate and accessible way.

One of his presentations, prepared for the Mental Health Social Care Strategic Network in which I was fortunate to participate, was titled 'Something Deep Inside Me'. Peter believed that we need to reach the depths of the human soul to discover what makes us into authentic human beings. In this presentation Peter posed what he describes as the 'eternal questions':

■ Where do we come from?

■ Who do you think you are?

■ What are we doing here?

■ What meaning is there in mental and physical distress?

■ Is there such a thing as 'a good death'?

■ Is death a closed door or a gateway to another life?

Few people involved at a senior level in the delivery of human services have asked us to stand back and take a look at these inner, existential issues which influence our leadership practice. Peter has been one of them in recent times. For someone who was confronted by such a disabling illness, Peter's focus on issues involving death as well as life was remarkable. It is significant that his last major enterprise was to edit a book on spirituality in end of life care. By confronting and reminding us of these deeper issues we are reminded of our fragility and humanity in whatever situation in our work or elsewhere that we find ourselves.

A focus on the soul

As well as drawing our attention to these deeper issues, Peter reminded us of the importance of the soul in guiding our inner selves. I have found relatively few references to the significance of the soul in the leadership literature, but Peter referred to 'soul filled leadership' as being an essential ingredient to a fully human approach for those of us in leadership positions. He related the 'soulful' organisation to a holistic view of organisational health through Plato's maxim: *'You shall not cure the body without the mind, nor the mind without the soul, because the part can never be well unless the whole be well'* (Gilbert, 2010).

Peter also referred to the insights of major religious traditions: *'This individual soul is unbreakable and insoluble, and can be neither burned nor dried. The soul is everlasting; present everywhere, unchangeable, innumerable and eternally the same... Knowing this, you should not grieve for the body'* (Bhagavaga Gita 2.23–25).

In Jewish thought, as Peter pointed out (Gilbert, 2013), there is a distinction between the 'soul', *nephesh*, and 'spirit', *ru'auch*. The soul is God-given, but passive; while the spirit is active as 'invigorated life'. In secular terms we also speak of 'soul' being a deep value-base in a person, while 'spirit' we use in terms of active inspiration.

For Peter the organisational 'soul' is seen as essential to the maintenance of the health and well-being of the organisation. He linked the lack of 'soul' to poor dysfunctional behaviour and poor clinical practice and has been particularly vocal in linking this to crises in health sector organisations, for example those encountered in Mid-Staffordshire. *'The soul-less organisation stifles creativity and initiative, and is fiercely resistant to challenge'* (Gilbert, 2010). He remarks pithily that the *'soulless leader rises without trace'* (Gilbert, 2010).

As discussed elsewhere in this book, Peter developed the theme of 'soul filled' leadership into a checklist for leaders to question themselves about their humanity as well as their effectiveness. He placed a particular focus on the importance of narrative and stories as being essential ingredients of leadership. He writes: *'Leaders in management roles need to listen to people's stories: users, carers, frontline staff, and weave these into an integrated narrative. This is what the great leaders of the ancient world did, and our need for stories continues'* (Gilbert, 2010). Peter believed that if these maxims had been followed, the dysfunctional nature of some NHS organisations, which led to shortcomings in standards of care, could have been avoided.

Compassion and love as essential ingredients in care

Alongside references to the soul and the need for organisations to be 'soulful', Peter referred frequently to the need for the values of compassion and love to be embedded into daily practice in health and social care. Margaret McGettrick elsewhere in this book refers to the way in which compassion in care is an essential element in practice in line with Peter's own philosophy. Peter quoted Sharon Salzberg: *'Compassion is not at all weak. It is the strength that arises out of seeing the true nature of suffering in the world. Compassion allows us to bear witness to that suffering, whether it is in ourselves or others, without the fear; it allows us to name injustice without hesitation, and to act strongly, with all the skill at our disposal* (Salzberg, 2002).

Peter also made frequent reference to love as being a core component of care practice. He quoted Chris Cook *et al* (2009): *'Doctor and patient are in complementary roles – both need the other. Indeed, at heart we are far more alike than we are different, and as we meet on the path of life, there is one medicine constantly at our disposal that even comes free. This is the power of love, lending hope, giving comfort and helping bring peace to the troubled mind.'*

Peter wanted to ensure that these core human values should inculcate an organisation which would otherwise become 'soulless'. In his career he experienced times when organisations forgot these core values, for example during the Staffordshire 'pindown' crisis when poor and abusive childcare practice in the county's residential establishments was exposed. He was determined that the lessons learnt should not be forgotten.

Leadership and religious traditions

As we have been reminded elsewhere in this book, Peter's work and his thinking were deeply influenced by his religious roots and in particular by his integration of the principles of the Benedictine rule to everyday leadership practice. The Benedictine rule urges us to *'listen with the ear of the heart'*, and the ethos is of a father or mother figure exercising 'servant leadership': *'Therefore, he must so arrange everything that the strong have something to yearn for and the weak nothing to run from'* (Rule of St Benedict, 64).

Peter also noted the special quality of the Dominican model: *'The genius of Dominic was that he devised a structure that respected the value of individual freedom, while at the same time safeguarding the survival and flourishing of both the local communities and the Order as a whole'* (Dorr, 2006). A theme which influenced Peter throughout his career is that of servant leadership. This runs equally through other traditions for example, the leader of the Sikh community in Soho Road, Birmingham, is called Bhai Sahib – brotherly leader.

The legacy of Peter's background and work will be to see leadership as an essentially 'humanising' endeavour. He drew attention to the maxim to 'be yourself more, with skill' and he referred to the need to put 'we before me', and to think and act for the longer term. Authenticity in leadership was also a key theme for him.

The influence of contemporary thought on Peter's work

Peter's contribution to the themes in this book were shaped not just by his own Benedictine roots, but equally by a number of modern seminal thinkers. He was convinced that so much of the lives of those who live in care settings, as well as those who care for them, lack meaning and purpose. He liked to quote Viktor Frankl's reflections after years of reflection on what brings meaning and purpose in life: *'Man is not destroyed by suffering – he is destroyed by suffering without meaning'* (Frankl, 1984).

Peter was much influenced by Jonathan Sacks' view that we are all meaning-seeking creatures if we are to make any sense of the world: *'The search for God is the search for meaning … And that is no small thing, for we are meaning-seeking animals. It is what makes us unique. To be human is to ask the question, 'why?''* (Sacks, 2011).

Another contemporary thinker, Zygmund Bauman, encapsulated for Peter much of the angst of modern society when he described: *'The new individualism, the fading of human bonds and the wilting of solidarity'* (Bauman, 2006).

Peter felt this 'new individualism' keenly, particularly over the last few years. He referred to the 'CBT panacea' as representing an overly individual view of human nature. He referred us to Aristotle's view that happiness is not an individual aspect of humanity but is essentially about human 'flourishing', which was to do with our positive interaction with other human beings.

Peter was not content just to theorise about these issues or leave them as some kind of intellectual parlour game. For him, they were the core dilemmas which touch the lives not just of service users, but of those caring for them. If staff have difficulty in thinking about their 'inner selves', they are unlikely to be able to persuade service users to do likewise.

As mentioned elsewhere in this book, Peter's passionate commitment to chaplaincy and spiritual care in mental health services, taken forward in recent years through the National Spirituality and Mental Health Forum, were about giving all staff and volunteers, not just professional chaplains, the tools to feel confident to conduct these deeper conversations and to understand the spiritual needs of those with whom they come into contact. As the newly elected co-chair of the Forum, I feel inspired by his work and legacy to ensure that his contribution to spiritual care is not forgotten.

In his conversations with myself and colleagues, Peter talked about the need to bring these issues to the fore in the world of social care as well as healthcare. In his annual retreats held in recent years in Worth Abbey for those involved in health and social care leadership and practice, he was able to provide participants with a deep sense of purpose and commitment in the return to daily practice. His residentials in the same setting in Worth Abbey for those involved in social care in mental health services, described elsewhere in this book by Hari Sewell, were an opportunity to bring fresh perspectives to the complex and often bewildering world of the interface of health and social care.

In my own role in providing pastoral care in hospital wards and residential settings, I come across communities of residents whose lives are spent looking at each other, perhaps pondering these issues, but not being given permission to express them. Their lives are often conducted in what might be seen as a 'liminal' existence'. This problem was summed up for me at a recent visit by the manager's parting comment: 'Just why are our residents always so morose?'

In the last few years Peter was particularly supportive in my work in developing awareness of understanding and meeting the spiritual needs of people with dementia.

Spirituality and end of life care

I think it is no accident that Peter felt impelled to devote his last magnum opus to the theme of spirituality and end of life care. His editing of *Spirituality and End of Life Care* (2013) started just prior to receiving the diagnosis that he was suffering from the terminal condition motor neurone disease. How much we admire his courage and determination in continuing with and completing this herculean task in the knowledge of his own disability and life-threatening condition.

Those of us who have contributed to this book feel a sense of privilege to have taken part in this unique project. It will be a legacy in translating Peter's deeper concerns about the human condition into tangible and practical benefits for both service users and those close to them, as well as staff and volunteers.

Peter never avoided difficult and complex issues. In *Spirituality and End of Life Care* (2013) he poses a seemingly brutal question in his introduction. In end of life care, are we referring to a 'rage against the dying of the light', or 'a new light shining'? He refers to our society as being 'necrophobic' and that part of our dilemma is that we have tended to 'unmoor life from death'. He was convinced that we have to confront the realities of the end of life as much as we need to confront the realities of life itself.

He wrote of the contribution of the three Abrahamic faiths to our understanding of the end of life: *'The three Abrahamic faiths: Judaism, Christianity and Islam, envisage a process of judgment and an afterlife; an egalitarian process, where good deeds are recognised, but worldly status is irrelevant. Eastern faiths and philosophies such as Hinduism and Buddhism envisage a process of reincarnation and a move towards a state of perfection for the individual soul through a sloughing off of materialist pretentions.'* (Gilbert, 2011)

Peter always welcomed the insights of other cultures and he was particularly close to the Sikh community. He quoted the saying of the Gurus: *'The people in this world fear death and (try to) hide themselves from it lest death's courier should catch and take them away'* (Bakhshi, 2008).

The importance of dialogue across faith communities

Peter's knowledge of, and contact with, the major faith traditions showed his passion in seeking to take forward our understanding of the deeper issues in life. Equally important in his work is how we might encourage and empower service users to articulate and have the conversations that he so eloquently described. Peter's links with the Sikh community, particularly in Birmingham, demonstrated his commitment to taking forward his philosophy and guiding principles across faith communities. He was frustrated when encountering 'gatekeeping' in interfaith relations and was at his best when discussing issues around our inner selves in a multi-faith context. At an interfaith seminar he chaired in Birmingham at the Gurdwara in March 2010 I was somewhat lost for words when he turned to me and asked me: 'Ben, what does the Christian tradition say about our inner selves?'

In my end is my beginning

'In my end is my beginning'. These words, written by TS Eliot just prior to the Second World War, encapsulate the belief of many faith traditions in describing new lives and modes of existence after death. I think Peter would have agreed that while he was able to influence care practice and leadership practice with his ideas, there is still much work to be done. The work of countering reductive tendencies with a focus on the 'inner self' in an increasingly secular world will continue to be an important task for all of us committed to 'humanising' services.

Peter may have reflected in his work on the 'necrophobic' nature of our society but in his attitude to his own mortality he was anything but necrophobic. His funeral service was a clear and confident statement of his beliefs. He always encouraged us to confront issues of life and death in a clear and unsentimental way. Peter's contribution to the issues on which this book has focused – the contribution of spirituality to human endeavour – may have ended, but he challenges us to ensure that his work and focus is not left unfinished.

His focus on spirituality and its importance for humanity and its future will continue to inform us in many spheres of human services, not just mental health services but equally interfaith relations, social care and values-based leadership, about which he felt so passionate.

It remains for us to take forward Peter's contribution to these fields, both to seek new insights and more importantly to find ways of using these to enrich the lives of those with whom we come into contact with in our professional and personal lives. In this way we may be able to say that what seems to be an end approaching could be the start of a new beginning. Peter, in his life and work has always focused on the 'other side of the river'. Having now taken his own journey 'across the river' we need to take forward his legacy for the good of all the vulnerable and wounded people whom we meet in our daily lives and for whom Peter was so concerned.

References

Bakhshi SS (2008) *A Modern Guide to the Practice of Sikh Faith*. Birmingham: Sikh Publishing House.

Bauman Z (2006) *Liquid Fear*. Cambridge: Polity Press.

Cook C, Powell A & Sims A (2009) *Spirituality and Psychiatry*. London: RC Psych Publications.

Dorr D (2006) *Spirituality of Leadership, Inspiration and Empowerment, Intuition and Discernment*. Dublin: Columba Press.

Eliot TS (1943) *The Four Quartets*. New York: Harcourt, Brace and Co.

Frankl V (1984) *Man's Search for Meaning*. New York, NY: Simon & Schuster.

Gilbert P (2010) *Something Deep Inside Me: Presentation prepared for the Annual Residential of the Social Care Strategic Network*.

Gilbert P (2011) *Spirituality and Mental Health*. Brighton: Pavilion Publishing.

Gilbert P (2013) *Spirituality and End of Life Care*. Hove: Pavilion Publishing.

Sacks J (2011) *The Great Partnership: God, science and the search for meaning*. London: Hodder and Stoughton.

Salzberg S (2002) *Lovingkindness: The revolutionary art of happiness*. Boston: Shambhala Classics.

Further reading

Books and monographs

Gilbert P (1979) (with Dr Peter Dickens) *The State and the Housing Question: A local study and some wider issues*. Brighton: University of Sussex Monograph.

Gilbert P (1985) *Mental Handicap: A practical guide for social workers*. London: BPI.

Gilbert P & Scragg T (1992) *Managing to Care*. London: BPI.

Gilbert P (2003) *The Value of Everything: Social work and its importance in the field of mental health*. Lyme Regis: Russell House Publishing.

Gilbert P (2005) *Leadership: Being effective and remaining human*. Lyme Regis: Russell House Publishing.

Coyte ME, Gilbert P & Nicholls V (eds) (2007) *Spirituality, Values and Mental Health: Jewels for the journey*. London: Jessica Kingsley Publishers. (Including writing chapters 1 and 10; 11 (with Wendy Edwards), and 17 (with Sarajane Aris)).

Gilbert P & Kalaga H (2007) *Nurturing Heart and Spirit: Papers from the multi-faith symposium*. Stafford: Staffordshire University/CSIP.

Gilbert P (2010) *Social Work and Mental Health: The value of everything, Lyme Regis: Russell House Publishing*. (Sole written chapters: 1,3,5,7,9,11 and 12. Chapter 4 written with Dr Michael Clark)

Parkes M & Gilbert P (2011) *Report on the Place of Spirituality in Mental Health*. London: National Spirituality and Mental Health Forum.

Gilbert P (ed) (2011) *Spirituality and Mental Health*. Brighton: Pavilion Publishing. (One sole chapter and 2 joint chapters)

Gilbert P (ed) (2013) *Spirituality and End of Life Care*. Hove: Pavilion Publishing and Media. (Two sole chapters)

Contributions to edited works

Chapter on the role of the social worker in Craft M, Bicknell J & Hollins S (eds) (1985) *Mental Handicap: A multi-disciplinary approach*. London: Bailliere Tindall.

Chapter for SPN national study day publication (2004) *Integrity and Integration in The Integration of Health and Social Care*. London: SPN. Study Day Paper 6.

Inaugural Professorial lecture in B Moss (Ed) (2005) *Explorations*. Centre for Spirituality monograph, Stafford: Staffordshire University, pp24–49.

Chapter on spirituality and mental health in J Cox, A Campbell and K W M Fulford (Eds) (2007) *Medicine of the Person: Faith, science and values in health care provision*. London: JKP, pp141–156.

Chapter for SPN national study day publication (2006) 'Breathing Out – Breathing In', in *Reaching the Spirit*, London: SPN. Study Day Paper Nine.

Chapter on Spirituality and Mental Health in T Basset and T Stickley (Eds) (2007) *Learning About Mental Health Practice*. Chichester: Wiley, pp531–555.

Chapter with Dr Sarah Eagger and Peter Richmond in C Cook, A Powell and A Sims (2009) *Spirituality and Psychiatry*. London: RCPsych (peer reviewed), pp190–212.

Chapter on Leadership in N Thompson and J Bates (Eds) (2009) *Promoting Workplace Well-Being*. Basingstoke: Palgrave Macmillan, pp103–116.

Chapter in *Words in Action in Ten Thousand Places*. London University: The Heythrop Series, Issue 12. [considering the interaction between faith communities and mental health services]

Chapter in T Basset and T Stickley (Eds) (2010) *Voices of Experience: Narratives of Survival and Mental Health*. Oxford: Blackwell/Wiley [relating to personal experience of mental illness to spirituality], pp95–114.

Chapter in J Atherton, E Graham and I Steedman (Eds) (2010) *The Practices of Happiness: Political economy, religion and well-being*. London: Routledge, pp157–169.

Chapter in H Sewell (Ed) (2012) *The Equality Act 2010 in Mental Health: A guide to implementation and issues for practice*. London: Jessica Kingsley.

Chapter in J Simmons (Ed) (2013) *Faith with its Sleeves Rolled Up*. London: Faith Action.

Articles

Gilbert P & Spooner B (1982) Strength in Unity: Community Teams/ *Community Care*, 28th October, 1982, pp17–18.

Gilbert P (2004) Every day is D-Day. *Care and Health*, June, 24–25.

Gilbert P (2005) Keep up your spirits (running, spirituality and mental health). *Open Mind*, 135, Sept/ Oct, 6–8.

Gilbert P & Sewell H (2006) Leading and learning. *British Journal of Leadership* **2** (1) 4–11.

Gilbert P (2006) Social care services and the social perspective. *Psychiatry* **5** (10).

Gilbert P (2006) Breathing space. *Community Care*, 19th January, 36–37.

Gilbert P & Watts N (2006) Don't mention God!. *A Life in the Day* **10** (3) 20–25.

Gilbert P (2006) We need leaders at all levels with heart and guts. *Open Mind* 138, March/April 16–17.

Gilbert P (2007) Spirituality: "Weasel-word" or gateway to new understandings. *Philosophy, Psychology and Psychiatry* **13** (3) 197–199.

Robb J & Gilbert P (2007) Leadership lessons in health and social care: mental health. *The International Journal of Leadership in Public Services* **3** (1) 17–25.

Gilbert P (2007) Nobody noticed: leadership and issues of workplace loss and grief. *Illness, Crisis and Loss* **15** (3) 219–231.

Gilbert P & Merchant R (2007) The modern workplace: surfing the wave or surviving the straightjacket? *Crucible* Jan–March 39–46.

Moss B & Gilbert P (2007) Flickering candles of hope: spirituality, mental health and the search for meaning. *Ilness, Crisis and Loss* **15** (2) 179–191.

Gilbert P (2007) Engaging hearts and minds….and the spirit. *The Journal of Integrated Care* **15** (4) 21–27.

Gilbert P (2007) Spirituality and mental health: a very preliminary overview. *Current Opinion in Psychiatry* **20** 594–598.

Nicholls V & Gilbert P (2007) The sea, me and God. *Open Mind* **144 March/April** 11–13.

Slay G & Gilbert P (2007) When the spirit is weak. *Professional Social Work* **February, 2007** 16–17.

Gilbert P (2008) Nurturing a new discourse: mental health and spirituality. *Spirituality and Health International* **June**.

Gilbert P & Kalaga H (2007) Believing in mental health (with Halina Kalaga) *Open Mind* **147 September/October** 8–9.

Gilbert P & Bates P (2008) I wanna tell you a story: leaders as storytellers. *The International Journal of Leadership in Public Services* **4** (2).

Hossain MS & Gilbert P (2010) Concepts of death: a key to our adjustment. *Illness, Crisis and Loss* **18** (1) 19–36.

Gilbert P (2010) Integrating a spirited dimension into health and social care. *British Journal of Wellbeing* **1** (3) 20–24.

*Gilbert P (2010) Seeking inspiration: the rediscovery of the spiritual dimension in health and social care in England. *Mental Health, Religion and Culture* **13** (6) 533–546.

*Parkes M & Gilbert P (2010) God and Gurdwaras: the spiritual care programme at the Birmingham and Solihull MHFT. *Mental Health, Religion and Culture* **13** (6) 569–583.

*Gilbert P & Fulford KWM (2010) Bringing the spirit and values back into public services. *The International Journal of Leadership in Public Services* **6** (2) 6–19.

Gilbert P & Parkes M (2011) Professionals calling: mental healthcare staff's attitudes to spiritual care. *Implicit Religion* **14** (1) 23–43.

Gilbert P & Clark M (2010) Making public services user focused: the history of NIMHE. *The International Journal of Leadership in Public Services* **6** (2) 25–38.

*Bolam S, Carr S & Gilbert P (2010) The Jersey Service User Participation Programme. *The International Journal of Public Services* **6** (2) 54–67.

*Parkes M, Milner K & Gilbert P (2010) Vocation, vocation, vocation: spirituality for professionals in mental health services. *The International Journal of Leadership in Public Services* **6** (3) 14–25.

Gilbert P, Parkes M & Kaur N (2010) Let's get spiritual. *Mental Health Today* **October** 28–33.

Gilbert P (2011) From the cradle – to beyond the grave. *Quality in Ageing and Older Adults* **12** (3) 141–151.

Gilbert P & Parkes M (2011) Faith in one city. *Ethnicity and Inequalities in Health and Social Care* **4** (1) 16–27.

Gilbert P (2011) I Robot: has the modern workplace lost its soul? *The International Journal of Leadership in Public Services* **7** (2) Second special edition with Professor KWM Fulford.

Gilbert P (2011) A pilgrimage in spirituality, mental health and wellbeing. *Open Mind* **Nov/Dec** 4–5.

Gilbert P (2012) Afghanistan – The 'Great Game' without End? *The International Journal of Leadership in Public Services* **8** (1) 56–69.

Gilbert P & Stickley T (2012) The wounded healer: education and the experience of mental ill-health' (with Dr Theodore Stickley). *Mental Health: Education, Training and Practice* **7** (1) Spring, 33–41.

Guest edited two special editions of peer reviewed journals in 2010: *Mental Health, Religion and Culture and The International Journal of Leadership in Public Services* (with Professor KWM Fulford) (Articles in the special editions marked with an *).

Guest edited a second special edition of *The International Journal of Leadership in Public Services*, with Professor KWM Fulford, June, 2011.

Guest edited a special edition of *Openmind*, with Jayasree Kalathil, Nov/Dec, 2011.

Handbooks and training packs

With Dr Neil Thompson: *Supervision and Leadership* (2002). Learning Curve Publications.

With Dr Neil Thompson: *Developing Leadership: A training and resource manual*, published July 2010.

Chapter: 'Introduction to Spirituality', in CSIP (2009) *Whole Life Workbook*, CSIP/Eastern Development Centre.

With Dr Neil Thompson: *Supervision Skills: A Learning and Development Manual*, 2011.

Input to Ben Bano's parish/deanery pack for the RC Church on understanding Mental Health, 2011.

DVDs

From the *Cradle to Beyond the Grave?* DVD of the 2nd national multi-faith conference at Staffordshire University, January, 2008.

National policy papers

Joannides D & Gilbert P (2003) *Briefing for the Directors of Social Services on the Integration of Mental Health Services: Positive Approaches to the Integration of Health and Social Care in Mental Health*. ADSS/NIMHE, October 2003.

Gilbert P & Nicholls V (2003) *Inspiring Hope: Recognising the importance of spirituality in a whole person approach to mental health*. NIMHE/MHF. November 2003.

Gilbert P (2008) *Guidelines on Spirituality for staff in Acute Care Services* (mental health), Staffordshire University/NIMHE/CSIP (with an online research findings by Merchant R, Gilbert P, and Moss B), October, 2008.

Allen R, Gilbert P & Onyett S (2009) *Leadership for Personalisation and Social Inclusion in Mental Health* (with Dr R. Allen and Professor S. Onyett). London: SCIE, Position paper 27, November, 2009.

ADASS Briefing paper on spirituality and mental health, June, 2011.

Input into:

The Chief Mental Health Nurse's report for the Department of Health, *Values into Action*, 2006.

The Public Health and Mental Health, DH policy report in March, 2010: *Confident Communities, Brighter Futures: A framework for developing well-being*.

The Ministry of Justice's NOMS programme: *Belief in Change Programme*, approved July 2010.

The National Mental Health Development Unit's Equalities Programme Board (DH) work on the equalities agenda.(Work, eg guidelines quoted in the March 2011 publication: *Do You See Me?: Recognising, understanding and caring for people with dementia, depression and delirium.*

Contribution to The Higher Education Academy/mhhe/SWAP, *Developing emotional Intelligence, resilience and skills for maintaining personal wellbeing in students of health and social care*, June 2011.

National conferences

Breath of Life: a national NIMHE/Pavilion conference on spirituality and mental health (2003).

Drinking from the Wells of Our Humanity (2004) NIMHE/MHF/Pavilion.

Nurturing Heart and Spirit (2006) Staffordshire University/NIMHE/National Forum.

From the Cradle to Beyond the Grave (2008) Staffordshire University/NIMHE/National Forum.

The Flourishing City: The role of spirituality in regeneration (2009) Staffordshire University/NIMHE/National Forum.